**Kindergarten-
1st Grade**

Po[...]

Ready, Set,
Show What
You Know™

Building Skills for
Ohio Proficiency Tests

Written By:
Andrea Karch Balas MS, MA
Judy Cafmeyer

Illustrated By:
Joseph Humphries

Englefield and Arnold, Inc. P.O. Box 341348, 6344 Nicholas Drive,
Columbus, OH 43234-1348
1-877-PASSING (727-7464) • (614) 764-1211 • Fax: (614) 764-1311
webpage: www.eapublishing.com
email: eapub@eapublishing.com

05 04 03 02 01 00   20 19 18 17 16 15 14 13 12 11 10 9 8 7 6 5 4 3 2 1

ISBN   1-884183-36-0

Englefield and Arnold, Inc.
P.O. Box 341348, 6344 Nicholas Drive
Columbus, OH 43234-1348
1-877-PASSING (727-7464) • (614) 764-1211 • Fax: (614) 764-1311
webpage: www.eapublishing.com

Englefield and Arnold, Inc. © 2000

Acknowledgements

Englefield and Arnold Publishing acknowledges the following for their efforts in making this proficiency material available for Ohio students, parents, and teachers:

Cindi Englefield Arnold, President/Publisher
Eloise Boehm-Sasala, Vice President/Managing Editor
Mercedes Baltzell, Associate Editor
Joseph Humphries, Illustrator/Cover Designer

About the Authors:

Andrea Karch Balas, MS, MA, is an educator and a scientist who has taught both in the traditional classroom and in nonformal educational settings, from kindergarten to adult. Andrea has presented nationally and internationally her research on the teaching and learning of science, including integrating science into all subject areas of school curriculum. She is currently supervising student teachers in a Masters of Education program, and is a doctoral candidate at The Ohio State University.

Judy Cafmeyer has taught for seventeen years in public and private schools from kindergarten to eighth grade. She is currently a proficiency workshop presenter and educational author for Englefield and Arnold Publishing, and is a reporter for *the Ohio Proficiency Press*. A graduate of The Ohio State University with a degree in elementary education, Judy has experienced education from various vantage points: as a teacher, on district curriculum committees, as a parent, a volunteer, and as a school board officer.

Teacher Reviewers:
Tonya Hawk
Sara Keaney
Mary Sasala

Table of Contents

Englefield and Arnold, Inc. © 2000

Englefield and Arnold, Inc. © 2000

Introduction

Welcome to this first in a series of *Ready, Set, Show What You Know*™ materials designed to begin preparing early elementary students for Ohio proficiency tests. The main focus of this K-1 edition is to offer a variety of thematic lessons and integrated activities that are aligned to the learning outcomes developed by the Ohio Department of Education for fourth grade.

These learning outcomes define the objectives and skills necessary for students to master by the end of fourth grade. With that in mind, the authors of *Ready, Set, Show What You Know*™ K-1 have modified the fourth grade learning outcomes to reflect primary building skills in the early education years. Lessons and activities contained in this book also demonstrate how teachers might use their K-1 curriculums and coordinate them to this modified version of Ohio's learning outcomes.

The fourth grade proficiency tests represent accumulated skill building that starts in the early elementary grades. Recognizing and practicing skills and strategies in Kindergarten and First Grade will help provide students with a foundation for future academic building blocks.

Writing

STRAND I - CONTENT

Ability to convey a message with supporting ideas and examples.

1. Responds to the topic.
2. Uses some details to support the topic.

STRAND II - ORGANIZATION

Ability to think logically and present ideas clearly and effectively.

3. A response that has a beginning, middle, and end.

STRAND III - USE OF LANGUAGE

Ability to use expressive language.

4. Beginning to use a variety of words.
5. Beginning to use a variety of sentence patterns.
6. A basic awareness of word usage (vocabulary, homonyms, and words in context).

STRAND IV - WRITING CONVENTIONS

Ability to apply the mechanics of English.

7. Shows an awareness of beginning spelling patterns.
8. Legible writing in print.
9. Uses capital letters to begin sentences and for proper nouns, also uses end punctuation.

Englefield and Arnold, Inc. © 2000

Reading

STRAND I - CONSTRUCTING MEANING WITH FICTION SELECTIONS

1. Beginning to summarize a fiction text.
2. Use graphs and illustrations to interpret information.
3. Retell a fiction story or poem in own words.
4. Identify some vocabulary which adds meaning to the text.

STRAND II - EXAMINING/EXTENDING MEANING WITH FICTION SELECTIONS

5. Analyze the text, by examining the actions of characters, plot, and/or the problem/ solution.
6. Make an assumption (inference) from the text.
7. Compare and/or contrast characters, setting, or events.
8. Respond to the text.
9. Choose books related to specific purposes; finding information and/or extending a topic or theme.
10. Predict outcomes and/or actions in a fiction text.

STRAND III - CONSTRUCTING MEANING WITH NONFICTION SELECTIONS

11. Beginning to summarize a nonfiction text.
12. Use graphs and illustrations to interpret information.
13. Retell nonfiction information in own words.
14. Identify some vocabulary which adds understanding to the meaning of the text.

STRAND IV - EXAMINING/EXTENDING MEANING WITH NONFICTION SELECTIONS

15. Discuss major ideas of the text.
16. Analyze the text with compare and contrast, cause and effect, or fact and opinion.
17. Make some assumptions (inferences) from the text.
18. Respond to the text.
19. Choose books related to specific purposes; finding information and/or extending a topic or theme.
20. Predict outcomes and actions in nonfiction text.

Mathematics

STRAND I - PATTERNS, RELATIONS, AND FUNCTIONS
1. Sort and/or identify objects on multiple attributes.
2. Make generalizations and predictions by: determining a rule, identifying missing numbers in a sequence, and identifying missing elements in a pattern and justifying their inclusion.

STRAND II - PROBLEM SOLVING STRATEGIES
3. Represent problem solving situations using pictures, graphs, number phrases, and words.
4. Identify information needed to solve a problem.
5. Explain or illustrate whether a solution is correct.

STRAND III - NUMBERS AND NUMBER RELATIONS
6. Separate, combine, order, and compare whole numbers.
7. Identify fractional parts of whole objects or set of objects.
8. Add and subtract whole numbers and explain or illustrate thinking strategies for making computations.
9. Use the symbols <, >, = for comparing whole numbers, sets, and basic fractions.
10. Relate whole number value by counting, grouping, applying place value and translating words and symbols.
11. Add and subtract decimals related to money amounts.

STRAND IV - GEOMETRY
12. Understand symmetry, simple closed curves, and the ideas of interior and exterior.
13. Recognize parallel and intersecting lines in geometric shapes.
14. Determine the characteristics of two-dimensional figures and compare shapes according to their characteristics.

STRAND V - ALGEBRA
15. Demonstrate a keying sequence on a calculator or computer.
16. Model a problem situation using a number phrase/sentence and/or letters ($2 + 3 = x$, $x + 3 = 5$, etc.).

STRAND VI - MEASUREMENT

17. Use tools to measure lengths (U.S. standard and/or metric units) and recognize the positions of whole numbers on a number line or ruler.
18. Understand the use of coins and bills in a buying situation.
19. Choose applicable units to measure lengths, capacities and weights in standard measurements.
20. Identify the perimeter of simple straight line figures and regions.
21. Tell time on both digital and analog (face) clocks.

STRAND VII - ESTIMATION AND MENTAL COMPUTATION

22. Make estimates in addition and subtraction.
23. Round numbers and use multiples of ten to estimate sums and differences. Discuss whether estimates are greater than (>) or less than (<) an exact sum or difference.

STRAND VIII - DATA ANALYSIS AND PROBABILITY

24. Use a table to record, sort and interpret information.
25. Find simple experimental probabilities and identify events that are sure to happen, events sure not to happen, and those we cannot be sure about.

Citizenship

STRAND I - AMERICAN HERITAGE

1. Notice connections among events by: sequencing major events, examining time lines and identifying cause-and-effect relationships.
2. Identify and use historical information sources, maps, magazines, newspapers, globes, etc.
3. Relate major events and individuals to a time line.

STRAND II - PEOPLE IN SOCIETIES

4. Recognize that Ohio is made up of many cultural groups.
5. Show how different cultural groups helped Ohio's growth.
6. Identify or compare customs and traditions of Ohio's various cultural groups.

STRAND III - WORLD INTERACTIONS

7. Use a map key to locate major landforms and bodies of water.
8. Use maps to show physical differences between regions.
9. Identify Ohio on a map of the United States.

STRAND IV - RESOURCE ALLOCATION (DECISION MAKING AND RESOURCES)

10. Identify what is needed to produce goods and services for people.
11. Name some resources used to produce various goods and services.
12. Classify everyday economic activities as producers or consumers.

STRAND V - DEMOCRATIC PROCESSES

13. Show how government makes laws, enforces laws, and judges laws.
14. Know that Ohio's government provides services to Ohioans.
15. Know that local governments provide services to the people in towns, cities, communities, etc.

STRAND VI - CITIZENSHIP RIGHTS AND RESPONSIBILITIES

16. Recognize the difference between statements of fact and opinion.
17. Identify and assess group decision making and cooperative activities.
18. Identify rules that are fair and respectful to others.

Science

STRAND I - NATURE OF SCIENCE
Abilities and thinking habits in investigating science ideas.

1. Group objects according to shared characteristics.
2. Read or interpret data from graphs and take measurements.
3. Identify or compare objects (lightest, longest, smallest, tallest).
4. Use a simple key to distinguish between objects.
5. Analyze a series of simple daily or seasonal cycles.
6. Carry out a scientific exploration; gather information, perform experiments, interpret results, and draw conclusions.
7. Identify tools needed to collect certain scientific information.
8. Evaluate observations and measurements made by others.
9. Understand the safe use of materials in science activities.

STRAND II - PHYSICAL SCIENCE
Observation and exploration of simple physical principles.

10. Recognize some simple machines: pulley, wheel, axle, wedge, inclined plane, screw.
11. Identify a simple physical change as a change in size, shape (configuration), or state of matter.
12. Predict the motion of objects and effects on other objects.

STRAND III - EARTH AND SPACE SCIENCE
Fundamental concepts in geology and meteorology made by exploring effects through observation and inference.

13. Predict the weather from observed conditions.
14. Describe how human activity affects the environment.
15. Identify examples of changes in the Earth's surface.

STRAND IV - LIFE SCIENCE
Basic concepts that can be directly observed or explored.

16. Understand what is needed to keep something alive.
17. Recognize some reasons for environmental changes among plants and animals.
18. Identify differences of living and nonliving things.
19. Understand the importance of a healthy diet for humans.

How to Use This Book

This *Ready, Set, Show What You Know™* teacher manual presents a variety of activities spanning K-1 students' skills and developmental levels. The authors' intent was the creation of a format that addressed the educational diversity found in every classroom. With the variety of themed lessons and activities contained in this K-1 edition, teachers have a great deal of flexibility to adjust the materials to fit specific curricular requirements for any group of students.

The A-B-C format of this book is used as an organizational tool and does not indicate any chronological or hierarchical order of skill development. The themes and activities can be used anytime throughout the school year or even repeated as review in a particular area. The degree of skill mastery needed to complete the activities does not build throughout the text but maintains a broad, overall K-1 focus.

The themed activities are intended to enhance and complement any school's curriculum by providing:
- Twenty-four themed lessons and activities that highlight the five content areas of the Ohio Proficiency Test (Reading, Writing, Mathematics, Citizenship, and Science).
- Future Focus with questions or activities to use at another time to check whether students can apply the objective.
- Lessons and activities correlated to Ohio's fourth grade learning outcomes (modified version).
- Circle questions that accompany each themed activity. These questions familiarize students with the proficiency "filled circle" method for selecting an answer or making a particular choice. A reproducible template which displays a filled and an open circle is included in this Teacher book (page 112) and at the beginning of the Student Workbook.
- Student Polls in every Citizenship activity provide another opportunity to use the circle paddle for answer selections. It is recommended that poll results be tallied, totaled, and discussed for supporting and opposing viewpoints. This can give students the opportunity to justify and defend their individual responses in a group discussion setting.
- Teacher direction pages correspond to Student Workbook pages. Each teacher direction page has a mini-student page pictured for quick and easy referencing.
- Writing activities with pictures or words that recognize the scope of reading and writing skills in K-1 classrooms.
- Picture book references corresponding to each theme (fiction and nonfiction) to start, restart, or jumpstart a lesson or activity.
- Science experiments that are easy to use and K-1 classroom friendly.
- Xtra, Xtra offers additional teacher support with web site listings, a book list of additional selections that the authors found too good to pass up, and templates that are used for specific activities.

An AsSORTment of Apples

Objective   Sort and classify according to attributes.

Learning Outcomes   Mathematics 1, 3

Materials
- floor grid
- a variety of apples: different shapes, sizes, colors
- balance scale
- hand lenses

Procedure   Distribute an assortment of apples, so that each student or group of students will have one apple. Students will carefully examine their apples to determine distinguishing characteristics such as stems, leaves, bumps, bruises, and/or two-colors. Balance scales and hand lenses can be available for students to inspect their apples more closely. Make a large floor graph for categorizing the apples according to the identified characteristics. This can be accomplished with a large piece of roll paper and markers.

Follow Up
1. How many different categories are identified on the graph?
2. Which category contains the most apples?
3. Which category contains the least apples?
4. Are there ways (other than those listed) in which the apples can be grouped?

Future Focus   Are students able to observe other objects for distinguishing attributes? Can students use shared characteristics to sort and classify?

Circle Questions
	YES	NO
• Do you only like to eat red apples?	O	O
• Have you ever climbed an apple tree?	O	O
• Have you ever picked yellow apples?	O	O
• Is a green apple likely to be ripe?	O	O

Extend the Theme by Integrating Subjects

Writing
LO 1, 2, 3

This creative writing assignment might be a class activity with student responses dictated to the teacher, or students can work on their own. **Prompt: If I had _____ apples, I would...** Students can use pictures or words to complete the prompt. Ask students to justify their responses using details.

Mathematics
LO 4, 5, 9

- Use apples to create tangible sets for students to observe and manipulate numerical groups. Have students compare sets of apples using the symbols and language of equality terms: greater than (>), less than (<), and equal to (=).
- Use two different colored hoops to make a Venn diagram (see template on pg. 107). Ask students to compare and contrast different apple attributes.

Citizenship
LO 8, 16

Students will use a map of Ohio, the United States, or the world to locate where the apples used for this activity were grown (i.e., Ohio, Washington State, New Zealand). Find that city, state, or country on a map or globe. To further extend this activity, discuss which method(s) of transportation might be used for shipping the apples from origin to destination.

Student Poll - Yes or No - Apples are always shipped by truck. Tally the results and compare viewpoints.

Science
LO 1, 2,
3, 10

- Students can compare weights of different apples using balance scales.
- Plant different types of apple seeds and compare their growth. Chart the growth: _____days, _____weeks, _____months.
- Students can compare their apple graphs to other students' graphs in the class and provide reasons for why seeds are growing or not growing.
- Use an illustration or an actual apple juice press to discover the number of simple machines contained in the press.

Safety Tip! Always wash fruits and vegetables before eating them.

Englefield and Arnold, Inc. © 2000

Reading

What's So Terrible About Swallowing an Apple Seed
Lerner, Harriet Goldhor
© 1996
Themes: apples; honesty; sisters

Seasons of Arnold's Apple Tree
Gibbons, Gail
© 1984
Themes: apples; seasons

The Giant Apple
Scheffler, Ursel
© 1990
Themes: apples; giants

The Story of Johnny Appleseed
Aliki
© 1963
Themes: apples; tall tales

Apple Pie Tree
Hall, Zoe
© 1996
Themes: apples; seasons; trees

Albert's Field Trip
Tryon, Leslie
© 1993
Themes: apples; ducks; school field trips

Even More Stuff To Do!

- Introduce the concept of fractions by dividing the apples into fractional pieces (1/2, 1/3, 1/4).
- Make applesauce in a crockpot and enjoy the aroma as the apples cook. Use different varieties of apples (sweet and tart) and no extra ingredients.
- Visit an orchard or grocery store.
- Invite a produce manager to the classroom to talk about what countries apples come from during the year.
- Contact pen pals in other apple producing states. Exchange apple seeds and see if apple seeds from another state can be grown in Ohio.
- Is there a place around the school or in the community to begin planting an orchard using successful seedlings?

Student Workbook Directions

A1

Student workbook page A1

Follow Directions

Students will color and cut out the nine apples pictured in their workbooks according to the following directions: Color red, the apple with a leaf, the smallest apple, the group of two apples, and the apple with a worm. Color yellow, the apple slices, the apple with no stem or leaf, and the apple core. Color green, the apple with one bite taken out of it and the apple with a stem but no leaf.

Students' cut-outs can be used for a follow-up pictograph activity on Student workbook page A2.

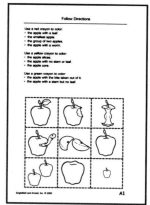

A2

Student workbook page A2

Graphing

Using the nine apple shapes from Activity 1, students will create a graph. There are three color categories on the bottom of the graph: red, green, and yellow. The vertical axis is numbered from one to four. Students will cut out the apples from the previous activity and paste each onto the graph according to the appropriate color.

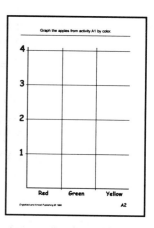

A3

Student workbook page A3

Writing

After creating a list of descriptive words with the class about apples (red, crunchy, sweet, etc.), use the apple-shaped writing paper to complete the prompt: **Apples are...**

Butter Blobs

Objective Evaluate a simple procedure to carry out an exploration.

Learning Outcomes Science 6

Materials
- 1 pint container whipping cream
- balance scale (optional)
- pinch of salt (optional)
- glass jar with lid
- measuring cup

- stopwatch (optional)
- teaspoons (optional)

Procedure Pour the entire contents of the whipping cream into a glass jar. Have students take turns shaking the jar until the cream separates from the liquid and a ball of solid butter forms. This activity can be done if students sit in a circle and pass the jar from one person to the next. Allow a specific number of shakes per person so that every student has a turn (i.e., five shakes).

Safety Tip! Make sure the lid on the jar is closed tightly.

Follow Up
1. Did all of the liquid become solid?
2. Could the size of the jar have an effect on the amount of time it takes for the change to occur?
3. How can we prove the guess (hypothesis) in question 2?
4. How will we measure the solid and liquid contents?

Future Focus Can students explain – with drawings, writing short sentences, or verbally – another simple physical change (i.e., water to ice), and identify what activity caused the simple physical change to occur (i.e., temperature or motion)?

Circle Questions

	YES	NO
• Does butter come from a cow?	O	O
• Could you make butter at home?	O	O
• Do you like the taste of butter?	O	O
• Is it likely that butter will melt on toast?	O	O

Extend the Theme by Integrating Subjects

Writing
LO 1, 2
- Retell or draw the steps used in the butter making process.
- Write a recipe for making butter.

Mathematics
LO 4, 19
- Use a stopwatch and time the number of minutes it takes to make butter.
- Measure how many teaspoons of butter are made from one pint of cream.
- If a second pint of cream is used to make more butter, will it take as long to make? Should you expect to get the same amount of butter as the first time? Explain your answer using pictures or words.

Citizenship
LO 17
Use The Butter Battle Book by Dr. Seuss to discuss how the two communities might have solved their problems. Next, have the students answer this question using pictures or words: **Why do you eat your bread butter side up or butter side down?**

Student Poll – Yes or No – Bread is eaten butter side up. Tally the results and compare viewpoints.

Science
LO 6, 11
Distribute ice cubes in cups or bowls to small groups of students. Ask students to observe and try to explain the simple physical change that takes place as the ice cube melts.

Safety Tip! Water makes a surface slippery.

Reading

From Grass to Butter
Mitgutsch, Ali
© 1972, 1981
Theme: grass turns into butter

Butter
Wake, Susan
© 1989
Theme: butter manufacturing

Peanut Butter and Jelly
Wescott, Nadine Bernard
© 1987
Theme: a play rhyme

The Butter Battle Book
Dr. Seuss
© 1984
Theme: accepting differences

Even More Stuff To Do!

- Put the butter on crackers and have it as a snack (butter side up or butter side down).
- Mold the butter into shapes using cookie cutters or candy molds.
- Invite a dairy farmer to speak to the class.
- Make seasoned butter by adding different herbs or spices.
- Discuss different ways that butter is sold such as whipped, sticks, and in tubs.
- Explain to students that butter makers are producers and butter eaters are consumers.
- Conduct a classroom poll to find "butter consumers" or "margarine consumers." What is the difference?

Teacher Notes

_____

_____

_____

_____

_____

_____

Student Workbook Directions

B1   Student Workbook Page B1

Beginning sounds – fill in the circle.

Fill in the circles for the items with the same beginning sound as the word "butter." Students will select from nine words: bubbles, bat, cat, wagon, kite, ball, bell, dog, chair. Encourage students to color the pictures.

B2   Student Workbook Page B2

Five-picture sequence

This page contains four pictures, each part of the grass to butter process. First, ask students to color each picture. Next, ask students to put the sequence of steps in the correct order by numbering each of the pictures in the top left corner. The fifth square, the last picture in the sequence, should be completed by the student. This square might include a picture of the student eating butter on bread or using butter to bake a cake.

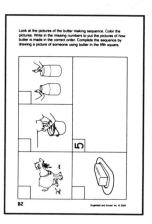

B3   Student Workbook Page B3

Yes/No selection response

Fill in the yes or no circle to designate your response to the cue: It's neat to eat...

1. butter blobs
2. butterflies
3. boxes
4. bottles
5. peanut butter
6. mushrooms
7. berries
8. bagels
9. bicycles
10. balloons

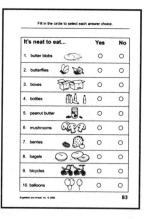

Cartography Configurations

Objective   Design simple maps to demonstrate map (cartography) skills.

Learning Outcomes   Citizenship 2, 9

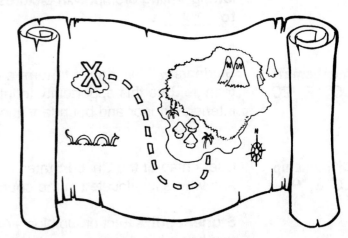

Materials
- treasure map (teacher designed)
- crayons
- treasure
- Ohio map (optional)

Procedure   A treasure has been hidden either in the classroom or on the school grounds. Invite students to suggest ways in which they might find this hidden treasure. After discussing the possibilities (hopefully using a map will be one of the suggestions), display your map and see if students can discover where the treasure is hidden. For the treasure, the teacher might have a special treat for the class, or a note announcing additional free or recess time.

You might have a variety of maps available for students to view, ranging from the simple treasure map, to a map of Ohio so they can find the location of their town, city, or village.

Follow Up
1. Brainstorm a list of map uses.
2. What are maps usually used for?
3. Was the teacher's map easy to follow?
4. What information is needed on a map?

Future Focus   Are students able to interpret the information on a map, key, and other symbols?

Circle Questions

	YES	NO
• Have you ever made a map?	O	O
• Have you ever used a map?	O	O
• Could you explain how to get to the Principal's Office?	O	O
• Have you ever seen a map of Ohio?	O	O

Extend the Theme by Integrating Subjects

Writing
LO 1, 3, 4

Students can develop a word list of people who use, or could use, maps in their occupations (jobs), i.e., bus drivers, surgeons (doctors), mail carriers, teachers. Using one of the occupations from the word list, complete the following writing prompt with pictures or words: **A _____ could use a map to _____.**

Mathematics
LO 12, 20

Students will join hands to form a circle or other shapes such as a square or triangle. Use this opportunity to introduce geometry concepts: perimeter, interior, exterior and boundary lines.

Citizenship
LO 8, 9

Use a map of the United States to have students identify the shape of Ohio and where it is located in the country.

Student poll - Fact or Opinion - All states have boundary lines. Tally the results and compare viewpoints.

Science
LO 5, 13

Have students look at a weather map from a newspaper. What information does the weather map reveal? Based on what they learned from the newspaper's map, students can design their own weather maps for the upcoming week.

Safety Tip! Review emergency evacuation procedures.

Reading

As the Roadrunner Runs: A First Book of Maps
Hartman, Gail
© 1994
Themes: animals; geography; maps; southwest

As the Crow Flies: A First Book of Maps
Hartman, Gail
© 1991
Themes: animals; city and town life; country life; geography; maps

My Map Book
Fanelli, Sara
© 1995
Theme: maps

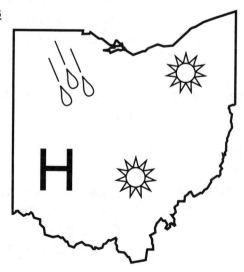

Englefield and Arnold, Inc. © 2000

Even More Stuff To Do!

- Use an internet map site to print a map from your school to the state capital in Columbus.
- Plan an imaginary vacation to a special interest place (i.e., Kings Island, Cedar Point, Sea World, Ohio Caverns) in Ohio and map out the directions.
- Have students take turns hiding a treasure in the classroom. Ask the student that hid the treasure to draw a treasure map for other students to use on their search.
- Draw maps to demonstrate how you can maneuver around the school. For example, how can you get from the classroom to the cafeteria or the gym?
- Use a map of the U.S. to show students how each state represents a different configuration (shape).

Teacher Notes

_____

_____

_____

_____

_____

_____

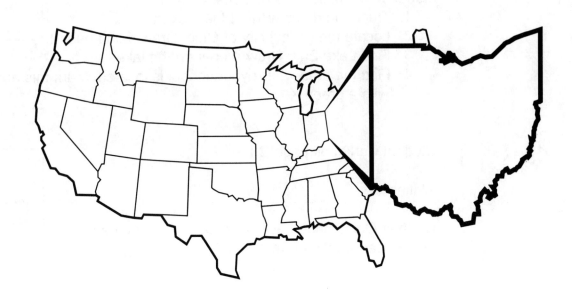

Student Workbook Directions

C1

Student workbook page C1

Following directions with follow up extended response.

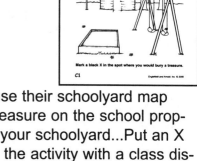

- Color the sandbox brown.
- Color the school house red.
- Color the swing set yellow.
- Color the leaves on the trees green.
- Color the trunks of the trees brown.
- Color the flagpole black.

After the directed coloring activity, students will use their schoolyard map activity page to show where they would bury a treasure on the school property. "You are in charge of burying a treasure in your schoolyard...Put an X where you would bury your treasure." Follow-up the activity with a class discussion: What kind of treasure would you bury in the schoolyard? What reasons can you give for burying your treasure in that spot?

C2

Student workbook page C2

Map recognition

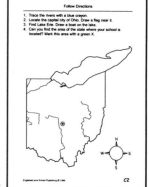

The Ohio map is separated into parts with rivers, Lake Erie, and the compass.

Using the map outline of the state of Ohio, give the students the following directions:
1. Trace the rivers with a blue crayon.
2. Locate the capital city of Ohio. Draw a flag near it.
3. Find Lake Erie. Draw a boat on the lake.
4. Find the area where your school is located. Mark this area with a green X.

C3

Student workbook page C3

Writing

On their Ohio shaped activity sheet, students respond to the open-ended prompt: **Ohio is...**

Dozens of Dandy Dandelions

Objective   Students learn about the life cycle of a dandelion and the sequencing of the dandelion cycle.

Learning Outcomes   Science 5, 16, 17

Materials
- dozens of dandelions in various states of maturity or pictures of dandelions in maturation sequence.
- paper, pencils, markers, crayons (optional)

Procedure   This activity may be done using live dandelions or pictures of dandelions. As a class, students will discuss the life of a dandelion. What are some clues to use to determine the life cycle? How does a dandelion begin? In small groups, students will sequence a set of dandelions (real or pictures). Discuss with students how they decided the sequencing.

Follow Up
1. Have you ever seen a dandelion?
2. Why do you think some places have dandelions and others do not?
3. Have you ever made a wish on a dandelion?
4. Do you know of any other plants that have flying seeds?

Future Focus   Are students able to draw a four to five-picture sequence illustrating other plant life cycles?

Circle Questions

	YES	NO
• Have you ever seen dandelions in the school yard?	O	O
• Are all dandelions likely to be yellow?	O	O
• Do you think a dandelion is a beautiful flower?	O	O
• Are dandelions weeds?	O	O

Englefield and Arnold, Inc. © 2000

Extend the Theme by Integrating Subjects

Writing
LO 1, 3

On a large sheet of paper make a class wish list. Have each child contribute one wish. Students will grant wishes for other classmates by completing the following prompt using pictures or words: **My wish for _____ is _____.**

Mathematics
LO 5, 22

- Working in small groups, have students try to estimate the number of seeds on the head of a dandelion. What is each group's estimate? Groups can compare their results. Were the students able to count the seeds?
- After blowing on a dandelion head, how many seeds are left? Use number phrases using greater than (>) or less than (<) to illustrate the comparison between the number of seeds on the dandelion head before and after blowing on it.

Citizenship
LO 16, 17

The class will take a poll to determine whether dandelions are considered flowers or weeds. To further illustrate the group decision making process, use the results of the poll to decide whether dandelions should be saved as flowers or eliminated as weeds.

Student Poll - Fact or Opinion - Dandelion bouquets are beautiful. Tally the results and compare viewpoints.

Science
LO 16, 17

Discuss as a class the following: How do dandelions disperse (send) their seeds (dandelions are flying seeds; dandelions are carried by wind)? Do all plants disperse their seeds like this? What might happen if you plant some dandelion seeds in soil? What is necessary for these seeds to grow?

Safety Tip! While many plants are edible, others are poisonous.

Reading

Dandelion Seed
Anthony, Joseph
© 1997
Themes: seeds; seasons; plants

Seeds on the Go
Fisher, Aileen
© 1977
Theme: seed dispersal

A Handful of Seeds
Hughes, Monica
© 1996
Theme: seeds

Englefield and Arnold, Inc. © 2000

Even More Stuff To Do!

- Take a walk around the schoolyard. Estimate the number of dandelions in the schoolyard.
- Make a list of suggested uses for dandelions.
- Pick a fresh dandelion and use it as a subject to make a painting. What colors will students use? Do they have to use the real colors of the dandelion?

Teacher Notes

Student Workbook Directions

D1   Student workbook page D1

Writing

On this page, students will respond to the prompt: **As dandelion seeds fly in the air...**

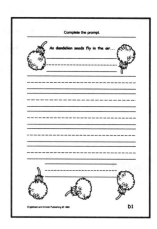

D2   Student workbook page D2

Taking a class poll

Take a class poll. How many boys have "given" or "not given" a dandelion bouquet? Write the number(s) for each category on the lines provided. Then, fill in the correct number of circles. Repeat this proceduce.

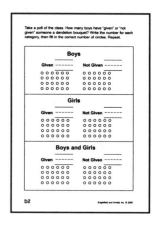

D3   Student workbook page D3

Color, cut, and paste a plant sequence using six pictures.

The bottom half of the page contains six pictures included in the life cycle of a dandelion. Direct the students to color the six pictures, then cut them out. Students should glue the pictures on the top half of the page in the correct sequence: roots, stem begins to appear, bud appears on the stem, open flower, seed head, seeds blowing in the wind*.

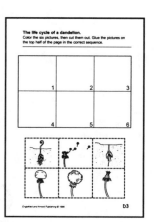

*Seeds blowing in the wind may also be the first step in the cycle.

                     Englefield and Arnold, Inc. © 2000

Eight Easy, Exciting Experiments

Experiment 1: What's in the bag?

Objective
Carry out a scientific exploration.

Learning Outcomes
Science 6

Materials
- brown grocery bag
- 3 objects for each group of 4-5 students (i.e., a potato, a pencil, and an aromatic candle)

Procedure
Students will use their senses (seeing, hearing, smelling, touching) to predict what is inside the sealed bag. Which sense is not being used? Why?

Safety Tip! Do not taste items used in science experiments.

Follow Up
Record your students' answers to the following questions:
1. When you look at the bag what do you predict or think will be in it? Why?
2. When you listen to the movement of things in the bag what do you predict or think will be in it? Why?
3. When you smell the bag what do you predict or think will be in it? Why?
4. When you feel the bag what do you predict or think will be in it? Why?

Extension
What is in the box? Place a sealed box with several objects contained in it on a desk. Can students predict what is in the box by just looking at the box? Are students able to eliminate items looking at the size of the box? What might students determine by shaking the box? Do not reveal the contents for a day or two or until the children correctly identify the contents. This activity can help students develop questioning skills and the process of elimination.

Experiment 2: Volcano

Objective   To observe an example of a physical change that has a potential impact on the Earth's surface.

Learning Outcomes   Science 12, 15, 17

Materials
- film canisters
- modeling clay
- vinegar
- baking soda
- red food coloring (optional)
- construction paper
- measuring spoon (teaspoon)
- plastic or styrofoam plate or tray as volcano base

Procedure   Students will mound modeling clay around the film canisters (one canister for each volcano, open end up) creating a triangular shape. Leave the top open. Decorate surrounding area with paper grass, flowers, trees, etc. Measure 1 teaspoon baking soda and put it in the bottom of the film canister. (If food coloring is being used - add it now.) Fill the canister with vinegar and watch for changes.

Safety Tip! Experiments are always performed with adult supervision.

Follow Up
1. Did anything happened to the environment around the volcano?
2. Were there any visible changes to the volcano?
3. What comparisons can be made between this experiment and a real volcanic eruption?
4. Are there volcanoes in Ohio?

Extension   Show a movie of a natural volcanic eruption.

Englefield and Arnold, Inc. © 2000

Experiment 3: Meteorology in the Making

Objective To analyze and predict daily seasonal changes.

Learning Outcomes Science 2, 5, 13

Materials
- paper plate
- brad fastener
- construction paper

Procedure Students will divide a paper plate into four equal parts. The class will select four weather symbols relating to the present season, such as clouds, a sun, snowflakes, or rain drops. These symbols will be drawn or pasted onto the paper plate, one symbol in each of the four sections. Students will construct a paper arrow and attach it with a brad to the center of the paper plate. They will place the arrow on their forecast for the next day's weather.

Safety Tip! Be prepared for seasonal weather changes.

Follow Up
1. Is it possible to predict the weather for the next week?
2. What clues can you use to predict the weather for the next week?
3. Are weather predictions usually correct?
4. How can you find out tomorrow's weather prediction?

Extension Plan a forecast calendar for next week or next month. Compare your forecast with the actual weather conditions. How accurate were your predictions in the comparison?

Experiment 4: Mighty Magnets

Objective   To group objects and create a graph to chart information.

Learning Outcomes   Science 1, 2, 3, 4

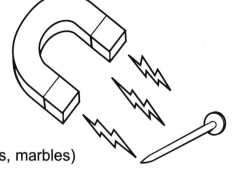

Materials
- a variety of magnets, different sizes and shapes
- an assortment of metal and nonmetal objects (coins, paperclips, pens, pencils, marbles)

Procedure   Children will observe the items and predict whether the objects may be attracted to the magnets. Students will then use the magnets to test which objects have magnetic attraction. Students can use their observations to begin a discussion about different metals and magnets.

Is there a magnetic attraction?		
Object	YES	NO

Safety Tip! Do not put magnets near computers or computer disks!

Follow Up
1. Do all magnets look the same?
2. Do different magnets attract the same objects?
3. Do magnets attract all metals?
4. Are metals always shiny?

Extension   Will a magnet attract an object through paper? wood? plastic? Predict and test. Students can make and test predictions about unknown objects and determine whether they will or will not be attracted by a magnet.

Englefield and Arnold, Inc. © 2000

Experiment 5: Classroom Derby

Objective   To recognize and use simple machines.

Learning Outcomes   Science 8, 10, 12

Materials
- an assortment of small cars and trucks
- triangular wood blocks

Procedure   Students will conduct a classroom car derby using toy cars and trucks. The cars will first be raced on a flat surface (floor or playground). Next, the vehicles will be placed on inclined planes (triangle wood block) and raced. Compare the results of the different types of races. Have students predict the outcome of each race. What might students expect to happen?

Science Tip! Be respectful when using other people's property.

Follow Up
1. What are the reasons that some vehicles go farther?
2. How did the inclined plane affect the race?
3. What other factors might affect future races?
4. Does a truck always race faster than a car?

Extension   Add extra weight (pennies or washers) to a vehicle and compare the result from that race to the result of the race with the vehicle that had no extra weight.

Experiment 6: I'm Real Fruity

Objective   To identify and compare objects.

Learning Outcomes   Science 1, 3, 6

Materials
- a variety of fruit seeds: apples, watermelons, peaches, plums, oranges, kiwi, grapefruit, cherries
- pictures of fruit, plastic fruit, or real fruit
- small spoons
- styrofoam bowls or cups

Procedure   Students will study the seeds and the fruits and try to match the seeds to the fruits.

Safety Tip! Do not eat the seeds used in the experiment.

Follow Up
1. How did you match a particular seed to a fruit?
2. What information did you use to match the seed to the fruit?
3. Do any of the seeds look similar to each other?
4. Do you think the size of the seed determines the size of the fruit?

Extension   Make a Favorite Fruit Graph. Have the students bring their favorite fruits to school. Each child should bring in one type of fruit. List all the different fruits on a bar graph. Students can fill in a square to designate their fruit contributions. Tally the categories to see which fruit is the most popular. After completing the graph and washing the fruit, make a fruit salad for the class to enjoy!

Safety Tip! This experiment is OK to eat.

    Englefield and Arnold, Inc. © 2000

Experiment 7: Food Fit For A...

Objective   To understand the importance of a healthy diet.

**Learning
Outcomes**   Science 16, 19

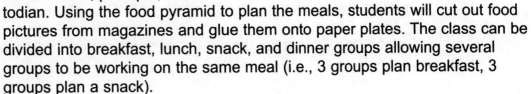

Materials
- food pyramid (Teacher's Edition, page 106)
- magazines
- paper plates

Procedure   Students will work in pairs or small groups and develop a day-long meal plan for an adult. This meal plan can be for a teacher, principal, cus-todian. Using the food pyramid to plan the meals, students will cut out food pictures from magazines and glue them onto paper plates. The class can be divided into breakfast, lunch, snack, and dinner groups allowing several groups to be working on the same meal (i.e., 3 groups plan breakfast, 3 groups plan a snack).

Safety Tip! Eat a variety of foods for a healthy diet.

Follow Up
1. Why is it necessary to eat a variety of foods?
2. What does food do for the body?
3. Are all foods healthy for you to eat?
4. What are your favorite foods?

Extensions
- Create a classroom food pyramid with magazine pictures.
- Identify student lunch choices on the food pyramid.
- Take a field trip to a restaurant.
- Invite a nutritionist to speak to the class about a healthy diet.

Experiment 8: Super Strength Seeds

Objective   To observe a simple physical change.

Learning Outcomes   Science 11, 12

Materials
- bean seeds
- film canisters
- water
- small plates or trays

Procedure   Students fill the film canisters with bean seeds. Add enough water to cover the beans inside the canisters and put the lids on them. Place the canisters on a tray and set aside. Watch periodically for changes to occur.

Safety Tip! Do not eat the seeds, drink the water, or disturb the canisters.

Follow Up
1. What do you expect to happen?
2. How long will it take? ___ minutes, ___ hours, ___ days?
3. Does this experiment compare to something else you have experienced (i.e., popcorn)?
4. Are the seeds still usable? Can you still plant them and expect growth?

Extensions
- Try the experiment with different kinds of seeds and compare the results.
- Plant some of the swollen seeds and record the growth for a specific amount of time (week, month, etc.). Plant dry bean seeds and compare their growth to the soaked bean seeds.

Englefield and Arnold, Inc. © 2000

Fact Finders

Objective Students will identify major ideas in a nonfiction selection.

Learning Outcomes Reading 13, 15

Materials • a variety of nonfiction materials

Procedure Read a nonfiction selection to the class and have students retell the facts of the story in sequential order.

Follow Up
1. What kinds of books or stories are not true?
2. What kinds of books or stories are true?
3. What kind of information would you find in a book about frogs?
4. What kind of information would you find in a book about you?

Future Focus Students are able to identify facts in a book or story.

Circle Questions

	YES	NO
• Are your height, weight, and age facts?	O	O
• Is it a fact that all puppies are cute?	O	O
• Today is Friday.	O	O
• Today is the best day of the week.	O	O

Extend the Theme by Integrating Subjects

Writing
LO 1, 2, 9

Students can use pictures or words to complete one of the following prompts:
- Four fun facts about Friday are _____.
- Five facts about February are _____.
- A faithful friend is _____.

Form complete sentences, beginning with capital letters and ending with punctuation marks.

Mathematics
LO 3, 10

Use manipulatives (domino-type) to introduce or review whole number addition and subtraction facts. The teacher will select a domino for students to illustrate and write a corresponding number sentence. For example, a domino showing three dots and two dots could be written as the number sentence: $3 + 2 = 5$.

Citizenship
LO 4, 6

Many people come from places all over the world to live in Ohio. What evidence is there to demonstrate that different groups of people have settled in Ohio? Students can brainstorm possible ways that prove other cultures have lived or are presently living in Ohio. For example, arrowheads and other Indian artifacts, different languages being spoken, etc.

Student Poll – Fact or Opinion – Facts can be proven. Tally the results and compare viewpoints.

Science
LO 3, 6, 12

Students will roll three different sized balls, one at a time, at a standing target and describe how the force of each sized ball affect the target. What results are expected if heavy-weight balls and light-weight targets are used? What about light-weight balls and heavy-weight targets? Does the amount of force affect the outcome? Have students guess and check.

Safety Tip! Be careful when throwing balls indoors.

Reading

Ohio Facts and Symbols
McAuliffe, Emily
© 1999

From Sea to Shining Sea: Ohio
Fradin, Dennis Brindell
© 1994

The following book is part of a series of books on the state of Ohio:
My First Book About Ohio! Why Wait to Learn About Our Great State
Marsh, Carol
© 1996

Englefield and Arnold, Inc. © 2000

Student Workbook Directions

F1

Student workbook page F1

Classification of items as living or nonliving

Direct students to look at the items listed. Students should fill in the circle to identify each item as living or nonliving.

1. money
2. ice cream cone
3. child
4. hat
5. sock
6. car
7. kitten
8. baseball
9. rocks
10. caterpillar

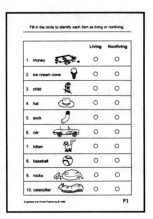

F2

Student workbook page F2

Writing

Students will complete each sentence by writing fun facts about their faces:
- I have _____ hair.
- I have _____ eyes.
- I have _____ nose.
- I have _____ ears.
- I have _____ _____.

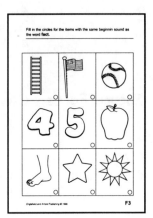

F3

Student workbook page F3

Beginning sounds – fill in the circle.

Fill in the circles for the items with the same beginning sound as the word "fact." Students will select from nine words: ladder, flag, baseball, four, five, apple, foot, star, sun.

Great Big Guesses

Objective   Use traditional and non-traditional tools and methods for measuring and estimating.

Learning Outcomes   Mathematics 17, 22, 23

Materials
- rulers
- yarn
- fishing line or heavy thread
- helium balloon
- roll paper

Procedure   **Day 1:** After reading or listening to a story about giants, children might discuss how tall they think a giant is: The giant is as tall as the ceiling or twice as tall as the teacher. Take a walking trip around the school to look at trees, the flag pole, school buses, or the height of the school. Record all of the things that the students have suggested for comparisons, along with whole number estimates on approximately how tall the objects are in inches or feet (i.e., 200 inches or 50 feet).

Day 2: The class will return to the objects they compared to the giant's height. With a helium balloon attached to a fishing line, measure the heights that were estimated from the previous day. In the classroom, students can use rulers to measure the length of the fishing line. The teacher (or other students) can demonstrate how the ruler measurements will convert into feet.

Follow Up
1. How many objects were found as giant comparisons?
2. Name some ways to measure things that seem impossible to measure.
3. Is it easy to estimate how tall a building is?
4. Would it be easier to estimate the size of small things?

Future Focus   Can the students make reasonable guesses when estimating?

Circle Questions

	YES	NO
• Do giants really exist?	O	O
• In your opinion, have you ever seen a giant?	O	O
• Have you ever seen a giant insect (bug)?	O	O
• Have you ever seen a giant animal?	O	O

Extend the Theme by Integrating Subjects

Writing
LO 4, 5, 6

Make a Giant (Big) Journal with two pieces of 12" x 18" manila paper folded in half, lengthwise. Students will keep a week-long log of their activities using pictures, words, or a combination of the two, in their unique diaries.

Mathematics
LO 17

Students lay on the gym floor feet to head. The teacher measures the length of the entire class with yarn. Float the helium balloon with the length of yarn in order for students to visualize the height of the entire class if they were standing on each others' heads. (This is a good activity to complete in physical education class.)

Citizenship
LO 14, 15

Suppose that a giant lives in the classroom. Make a list of rules that the giant must follow. Who will enforce these rules? Who will decide if the rules are fair? Will the giant receive any special privileges in the classroom? the school? the town? in Ohio? in the United States?

Student Poll - Fact or Opinion - Giants are real. Tally the results and compare viewpoints.

Science
LO 14, 15

Use your imagination and make a list of creative ways that a giant could alter (change) the Earth's surface. (i.e., When a giant cries, the tears will fill an ocean. When a giant sneezes, it can cause a windstorm.)

Safety Tip! Keep the planet clean.

Reading

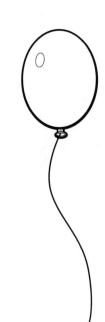

<u>Giant Hiccups</u>
Farley, Jacqui
© 1998
Themes: African-Americans; hiccups; problem solving; giants; food

<u>What Can a Giant Do?</u>
Cuneo, Mary Louise
© 1994
Themes: giants; size; stories in rhyme

<u>Mysterious Giant of Barletta: An Italian Folktale</u>
De Paola, Tomie
© 1984
Themes: giants; statues

<u>An Orange for a Bellybutton</u>
Fukami, Harui
© 1988
Theme: giant

Even More Stuff To Do!

- Working in small groups, students can create a large paper giant with separate body parts (head, body, arms, hands, legs). Each group can decorate a section of the giant and then it can be reassembled and displayed in the classroom or school hall.
- Shadow measuring: trace and measure students' shadows.

Teacher Notes

_____

_____

_____

_____

_____

_____

Student Workbook Directions

G1

Student workbook page G1

Identification of size

Students will color the biggest cat in the group yellow, then answer the questions on the bottom of the page.

G2

Student workbook page G2

Identification of size

Students will color the smallest dog in the group brown, then answer the questions on the bottom of the page.

G3

Student workbook page G3

Complete the bar graph

Students will complete the bar graph by coloring in the number of squares that correctly corresponds to each character's height.

- Boy: 3 feet tall
- Girl: 4 feet tall
- Dog: 2 feet tall
- Rabbit: 1 foot tall

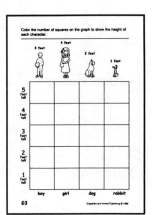

History is Happening

Objective

Create history while developing a classroom time line of events that are important to the students.

Learning Outcomes

Citizenship 1, 3

Materials

• newspaper
• crayons
• paper

Procedure

Use a newspaper to show ways in which special events in the school, community, state and world are collected and published for others to read about. Challenge students to become reporters and news gatherers. Select one day for each student to be the classroom reporter. As a class, discuss the notable events of the day or previous day (a birthday, a special guest, a favorite story read in the classroom). The reporter for the day will create a page for the class time line of special happenings. (The time line could be displayed clothesline-style using clothespins to add the continuing pages.)

Follow Up

1. What is an important event?
2. Who decides what is a news event?
3. When does history happen? yesterday? today? tomorrow?
4. Have you ever experienced a historic event?

Future Focus

Can students retell important events that occur throughout the school year?

Circle Questions

	YES	NO
• Has your picture ever been in the newspaper?	O	O
• Do you like to watch the news on T.V.?	O	O
• Have you ever been on television?	O	O
• Is the news on television always important?	O	O

Extend the Theme by Integrating Subjects

Writing
LO 1, 2, 3, 4

Prepare a daily, weekly, or monthly newspaper for the classroom on chart paper using everyday student happenings. Students can create a special title for the paper (i.e., Kindergarten Courier or First Grade Gazette). Include sections for different types of information such as special interests, sports, entertainment, or weather.

Mathematics
LO 6, 10

Use newspapers to locate and identify whole numbers. Give each student one newspaper page. Students will circle the whole numbers they find on their pages. As an introduction to the lesson, demonstrate how whole numbers are used in dates, advertisements, the sports section, etc.

Citizenship
LO 1, 3

Have students create a personal time line using information about themselves. Beginning with the day they were born, students will fill in three sequential events that have occurred during their five or six years of life.

Student Poll – Fact or Opinion – News is new. Tally the results and compare viewpoints.

Science
LO 6, 8

Create an "Invention Box" for the classroom. Students can work in small groups or independently. The box should contain a collection of odds and ends for students to explore and discover on their own. The objective for the students is to invent something. The completed invention should have a name and a purpose. Students should support their invention ideas with reasons for the discoveries. Their discoveries might result in "news" information for the day.

Safety Tip! Use classroom materials appropriately.

Reading

Rabbit's Good News
Bornstein, Ruth Lercher
© 1995
Themes: animals; rabbits; spring

Curious George Rides A Bike
Rey, H. A.
© 1952
Themes: bicycling; newspaper carriers; newspaper

Luck with Potatoes
Ketterman, Helen
© 1995
Themes: newspapers featured throughout; farm life; tall tales; fruits and vegetables

Student Workbook Directions

H1
Student workbook page H1

Create a classroom newspaper.

Each student will complete his/her page for the class-room newspaper. As a class, decide on the name for the newspaper. Write the name at the very top of the page. In the sections provided, students should write in the day's date and draw the current weather condition. A blank box is provided for students to draw pictures that correlate to the stories they write on the lines provided. The story can be about an event that happened in the classroom, in school, or at home.

H2
Student workbook page H2

Draw a symbol for each month of the year.

The months of the year are divided into two rows (the first six months and last six months of the year). As a class, decide which symbol best represents each month. Students should fill in the boxes accordingly.

H3
Student workbook page H3

Sequence of days, weeks, months and time

In relation to the day's date, students will circle the choice that correctly answers the following:

1. Today is: S M T W T F S
2. Tomorrow is: S M T W T F S
3. Yesterday was: S M T W T F S
4. This month is: J F M A M J J A S O N D
5. Next month is: J F M A M J J A S O N D
6. Last month was: J F M A M J J A S O N D
7. The time right now is: a.m.   p.m.

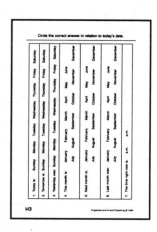

Introducing Inspector Inch

Objective   Recognize the inch as a small and basic unit of measurement in the United States.

Learning Outcomes   Mathematics 9, 17, 19

Materials
- Inspector Inch (Teacher's Edition, page 110 and Student Workbook, page I1)
- crayons
- pencils
- markers
- paper

Procedure   Inspector Inch will help students identify and investigate the inch as a basic unit of measurement. Students will use their Inspector Inch cutouts to measure and compare items that are greater than (>), less than (<), or equal to (=) an inch, in and around the classroom.

Follow Up
1. How many items were you able to find in the classroom that measured one inch?
2. Which is the smaller unit of measure: one foot or one inch?
3. How many Inspector Inches would it take to measure from your head to your toes?
4. How could you measure your foot?

Future Focus   Students can measure the number of inches in a foot and a yard accurately.

Circle Questions

	YES	NO
• Could this room be measured in inches?	O	O
• Would inches be the best way to measure the room?	O	O
• Would it take a long time to measure the room in inches?	O	O
• Can you think of a quicker way to measure the room?	O	O

Extend the Theme by Integrating Subjects

Writing
LO 3, 4, 6

Create a student-generated list of items that are approximately one, three or six inches in size. Post the word lists in the classroom for students to use when completing the following sentences using pictures or words:

- _____ is 3 inches long.
- _____ is 6 inches high.
- _____ is _____ long.
- _____ is _____ high.

Mathematics
LO 5, 9

Measure the different items students have listed in the Writing Activity as possible approximations of one inch. Were the objects greater than (>), less than (<) or equal to (=) one inch? Students might also illustrate some of the problems (i.e., a large paperclip > Inspector Inch).

Citizenship
LO 10

Inspector Inch wants to start his own business. What types of businesses do you think would suit Inspector Inch? How will he get started? Make a list of occupations that would suit Inspector Inch, then add the things that he will need to have to start that business.

Student Poll – Yes or No – Inspector Inch is very useful. Tally the results and compare viewpoints.

Science
LO 15

How might Inspector Inch's world be affected by different weather conditions such as rain, snow, or tornadoes? How do these conditions affect your world?

Safety Tip! A flashlight and extra batteries are useful for emergencies. Can you think of any other useful items?

Reading

Inch by Inch
Lioni, Leo
© 1960
Themes: birds; worms; measurement

Much Bigger than Martin
Kellogg, Steven
© 1976
Themes: measurement; growth

The following book is from the Math Counts book series that also includes Length and Capacity:
Weight
Pluckrose, Henry
© 1995
Themes: measurement; weight

Englefield and Arnold, Inc. © 2000

<u>Twelve Snails to One Lizard: A Tale of Mischief and Measurement</u>
Hightower, Susan
© 1997
Themes: beavers; frogs and toads; measurement

<u>Knee High Nina</u>
Kent, Jack
© 1990
Themes: adventures of size

Even More Stuff To Do!

Develop a story about Inspector Inch. You can use the story to develop a book for your classroom. Ask students the following questions (or make up some of your own!):

- Who does Inspector Inch know?
- How does Inspector Inch survive being such a small size?
- What does Inspector Inch eat? What does he do for a living?
- Make a home for Inspector Inch. What size will it be? What type of furniture can you find in his house?
- Who is in his family?

Inspector Inch might grow to different sizes after he visits his friend Wendell the Whale. Develop some stories the "larger" Inspector Inch might tell about all of the huge fish that he has seen (fish tales).

Invite the Music instructor to teach the class the song, "It's a Small World."

**Teacher
Notes**

_____

_____

_____

_____

_____

Student Workbook Directions

I1

Student workbook page **I1**

Color and cut out

Students should color and cut out on the dotted lines the three squares showing Inspector Inch and his vehicles. To facilitate use, it is recommended that you laminate all of these items. Inspector Inch could be mounted on a craft stick for easier handling.

1" Inspector Inch   3" car   6" boat

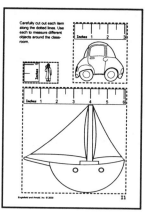

I2

Student workbook page **I2**

Measurement

Inspector Inch and his vehicles will be used to measure items in the classroom. For example, how many lengths of Inspector Inch does it take to completely measure the width of one's desk? Record the measure. Next, how many lengths of Inspector Inch's three-inch car does it take to completely measure the width of the desk? Record that number. When all measurements have been taken, compare results.

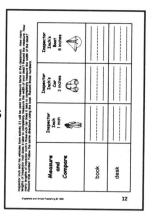

I3

Student workbook page **I3**

Equality symbols

The following items are listed: pencil, fingernail, paper clip, thumb, building block, glue bottle, crayon. Make sure items such as a paper clip, glue bottle, etc., are available to students. Using Inspector Inch, determine if each item is greater than (>) or less than (<) one inch.

Jack in the Book

Objective Examine the actions of characters named "Jack" in books, stories and poems.

Learning Outcomes Reading 5, 9, 10

Materials A variety of books and poems with characters named "Jack." See the book list on the next page under the Reading activity.

Procedure Students will listen to or read a variety of books, stories or poems with characters named "Jack." Use the literature selections to have students connect the characters and make predictions about actions or outcomes.

Follow Up
1. What was the story about?
2. Were there any other characters mentioned in the story?
3. Did Jack solve a problem in the story? How?
4. Would you like to read or hear another story about a character named Jack?

Future Focus Are students able to pick out main characters (people) in a story and identify the plot (the action, what happens)?

Circle Questions

	YES	NO
• Have you ever gone to a library?	O	O
• Do you have a favorite character in a book?	O	O
• Do you like poems?	O	O
• Do you know a poem that is also a song?	O	O

Extend the Theme by Integrating Subjects

Writing
LO 1, 2, 3

Students can use pictures or words to retell "Jack" stories substituting pictures of themselves or their names for the "Jack" characters. For example, "Mike" and the Beanstalk.

Mathematics
LO 3, 6

Count the number of times that the name "Jack" was used in a particular book, story or poem. Record the number of times that Jack's name or picture occurred. Compare the results to another book, story or poem with "Jack" as a character. As a class activity, graph the different "Jack" stories that were used in the classroom and record the results.

Citizenship
LO 1

Use some of the "Jack" books, stories or poems to identify cause and effect. For example, in the nursery rhyme about Jack and Jill, identify the cause and effect of the characters' actions.

Student Poll – Fact or Opinion – Jack characters are never heroes. Tally the results and compare viewpoints.

Science
LO 3, 6

Use a set of measuring cups to compare the weights for wet and dry materials. For example, students will weigh one cup of water and one cup of oatmeal. Do the two items weigh the same amount? How about 1/3 cup of water to 1/3 cup of sand, etc.? Students will compare their results.

Safety Tip! Be careful not to spill when using containers of water.

Reading

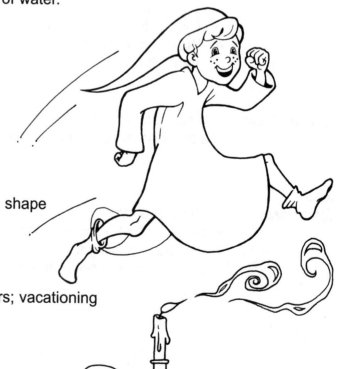

Meg and Jack Are Moving
Dowling, Paul
© 1990
Theme: moving

Meet Jack Appleknocker
Sundgaard, Arnold
© 1988
Themes: days of the week; shape

Hannah and Jack
Nethery, Mary
© 1996
Themes: cats; grandmothers; vacationing

The World That Jack Built
Brown, Ruth
© 1991
Themes: imagination; planning

Reading Continued

Jack and Jake
Aliki
© 1986
Themes: brothers and sisters; identity; twins

Mouse That Jack Built
Skekeres, Cindy
© 1997
Themes: cumulative tales; stories in rhyme; snowmen; mice

Even More Stuff To Do!

Involve parents and grandparents in the classroom by having students write letters asking them to make audio tapes of books, stories or poems. They may include some that were their favorites when they were in grade school.

Teacher Notes

_____

_____

_____

_____

_____

_____

Student Workbook Directions

J1

Student workbook page J1

Writing

Students will write short stories in which they are the main characters. They should draw a picture of themselves at the top of their page and write their stories on the lines below.

J2

Student workbook page J2

Yes/No circle questions

Students will develop chart information about themselves. To respond, each student should fill in the appropriate circle. Students will respond yes or no to the following questions:

1. I am a boy.
2. I am a girl.
3. I have a brother.
4. (not listed)
5. I have a sister.
6. I have a pet.
7. I ride the bus to school.

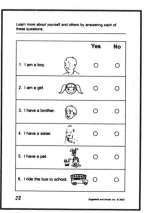

J3

Student workbook page J3

Using the information from the activity J2, students will complete their bar graphs.

Read aloud each sentence from activity J2. Ask students to raise their hands if they answered "yes." Students will fill in the circles for the number of "yes" responses to each statement. Students should then write in the total number of students that answered "yes" to the sentence. Follow this procedure for each statement.

Keying in on Clues

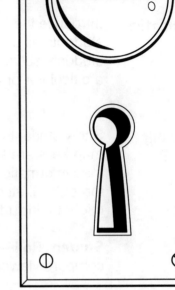

Objective   Create context word clues for solving riddles.

Learning Outcomes   Writing 3, 5, 6

Materials
- magazines
- scissors
- glue
- pencils
- paper
- hole punch

Procedure   Demonstrate to students the importance of key words and key information by playing, "What's behind the door?" Decorate a piece of construction paper to resemble a door with an ornate key plate and a keyhole (Use a hole punch to make a small keyhole). Place an object, or a picture of an object, behind the door. Give clues to have students guess what might be behind the door. For example, "It is red. It is round. It is made of rubber." If students haven't guessed the item with the clues given, allow them to peek through the key hole.

Follow Up
1. What is a clue?
2. What makes a good clue?
3. How much information should you give in a clue?
4. How many clues are needed to solve a mystery?

Future Focus   Students are able to identify important (key) information needed to solve riddles.

Circle Questions

	YES	NO
• Have you ever played a game using only clues?	O	O
• Did you ever give anyone a clue about a special gift?	O	O
• Would you ever use a clue to solve a mystery?	O	O
• Have you ever solved a mystery using clues?	O	O

Extend the Theme by Integrating Subjects

Writing
LO 3, 4, 5

Students will compose simple riddles using pictures or words to develop the clues.

Mathematics
LO 15

Introduce the buttons on a calculator or computer as "keys." Demonstrate to students all of the steps in an addition or subtraction keying sequence. Can students solve an addition or subtraction problem by repeating the steps on a calculator or computer?

Citizenship
LO 7, 9

Show students a map of Ohio and the United States. Point out where the map keys are located. Explain that the purpose of the key is to give special map information. For example, what might pictures of pine trees indicate (a forest)? Sketch a map of the classroom and have students suggest what might be included on this map key.

Student Poll – Yes or No – Keys always unlock things. Tally the results and compare viewpoints.

Science
LO 6, 8

Provide each student with a 3" x 3" piece of construction paper with a hole near the center (use a hole punch). Students can decorate around the hole to create a fancy keyplate. Then, have students view their surroundings through the keyhole. Describe how it is the same or different than looking at the entire picture.

Safety Tip! Use eye protection while performing science experiments.

Reading

<u>Lost and Found</u>
Teague, Mark
© 1998
Themes: school; hats; luck

<u>Dark Cloud Strong Breeze</u>
Patron, Susan
© 1994
Themes: locks and keys; cumulative tales; helpfulness

<u>A Dark Dark Tale</u>
Brown, Ruth
© 1981
Themes: mystery; large mysterious door

Reading Continued

Old Man and His Door
Soto, Gary
© 1996
Themes: misunderstanding; parties; Spanish language

Slinky Malinky, Open the Door
Dodd, Lynley
© 1994
Themes: misbehavior; stories in rhyme; cats; parrots; parakeet

What Am I?
Charles, N.N.
© 1994
Themes: cut out shapes; rhyming clues

Even More Stuff To Do!

- Students will create a door with a keyhole as a cover for a story. On a second sheet of paper, students will write about what is behind their doors. Attach the two papers either left to right, right to left, bottom to top, or top to bottom, depending on how they would like their doors to open.
- Invite the Music teacher to explain how the keys on a piano are used.

Teacher Notes

_____

_____

_____

_____

_____

Student Workbook Directions

K1
Student workbook page K1

Matching

Students will fill in the circle to indicate which keyhole matches the shape on each key.

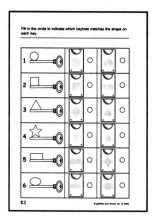

K2
Student workbook page K2

Compare simple keys

Students will study Key 1 and Key 2, as well as the picture of the bird. They will use this information to complete the following:

Use a filled circle to indicate which key describes the picture? Key 1 or Key 2

What does the other key describe?_____(a dog)_____

K3
Student workbook page K3

Sequencing (Patterning)

Students will use the correct letter from the simple key to complete each pattern.

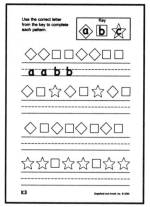

Lucky, Lucky, Ladybugs

Objective   Introduce students to four symbols that are identified with the state of Ohio.

Learning Outcomes   Citizenship 17, 18

Materials
- Teacher sheet (Teacher's Edition, page109) with Ohio symbols including the outline of the state, ladybug, buckeye, cardinal.

Procedure   Students will discuss different symbols that are associated with the state of Ohio and make a matching game using four state symbols: state shape, ladybug, cardinal and the buckeye. After coloring and cutting apart their eight game pieces (two of each kind), the class will decide on the rules that will be used for playing a matching game. This can be played by matching pairs alone, with a partner, or as teams. What other games can be developed?

Follow Up
1. Are you able to identify Ohio by its shape?
2. What might be a reason that ladybugs, cardinals, and buckeyes are used to represent Ohio?
3. Can you find Ohio on a map of the United States?
4. Can you find Ohio on a globe?

Future Focus   Students will recognize these four state symbols throughout the year.

Circle Questions

	YES	NO
• Have you ever caught a ladybug?	O	O
• Are you likely to find ladybugs in the winter?	O	O
• Have you ever seen a cardinal in your yard?	O	O
• Have you ever traveled outside the state of Ohio?	O	O

Extend the Theme by Integrating Subjects

Writing
LO 1, 3, 5

After listening to some books, stories, or poems about ladybugs, create a story about a ladybug. Make a book cover for the story using a paper plate cut in half and a brad to connect the two pieces. When the pieces are opened, it becomes a ladybug in flight.

Mathematics
LO 12

To demonstrate symmetry (see butterfly shown below), students will fold a piece of drawing paper in half and paint a shape or object on the left side of their paper only. While the paint is still wet, they will fold their papers left to right and produce a mirror image on the right side of their papers. When dry, encourage students to create an original art object using additional media such as markers, crayons, or stickers to decorate their paintings.

Citizenship
LO 2

A trip to the library will combine Citizenship and Reading (9, 19) outcomes. Introduce the librarian as a resource person who can help the students find additional information about topics that interest them. For example: When did the ladybug become Ohio's insect? When did the buckeye become Ohio's state tree?

Student Poll – Fact or Opinion – Ladybugs are helpful to the environment. Tally the results and compare viewpoints.

Science
LO 14, 17

Discuss with the class possible contributions that the ladybug makes to the environment, such as eating undesirable insects from plants and adding color to the world. Why would some farmers and gardeners want to buy ladybugs?

Safety Tip! Do not harm ladybugs because they help the environment.

Reading

Ladybug, Ladybug
Brown, Ruth
© 1988
Themes: ladybugs; stories in rhyme

Grouchy Ladybug
Carle, Eric
© 1977
Theme: ladybugs

Ladybug, Ladybug Where Are You?
Szekeres, Cyndy
© 1991
Themes: ladybugs; mice; find the ladybugs

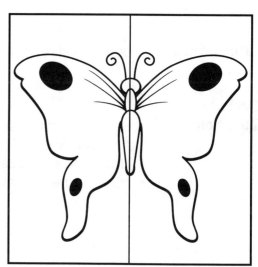

Even More Stuff To Do!

- Make up some symbols that can be specific to your classroom. Conduct surveys and vote on classroom favorites: colors, snacks, subjects, sports.
- Design a classroom flag or banner using the colors and symbols the class voted as their favorites. Display it in your classroom.
- Discuss non-edible fruits and plants such as the buckeye, poison ivy, toadstools.
- Prepare a class list of questions to ask the librarian about special topic items, i.e., ladybugs and buckeyes.

Teacher Notes

_____

_____

_____

_____

_____

_____

Student Workbook Directions

L1

Student workbook page L1

Three-In-A-Row

The top of the page is a nine square gameboard. The bottom of the page contains tokens for playing three-in-a-row: 5 ladybugs and 5 buckeyes. Students can color the tokens, then cut them out along the dotted lines. Discuss with the class the rules of three-in-a-row (the same rules as tic-tac-toe), and demonstrate the different combinations for winning the game. Students can then pair up and play three-in-a-row.

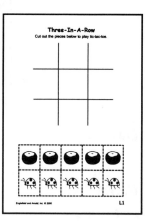

L2

Student workbook page L2

Sequencing (Patterning)

Fill in the circle to indicate the item that is next in the pattern.

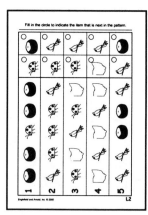

L3

Student workbook page L3

Simple addition

Students will count the number of dots on each ladybug and write that number on the line below the bug. Students will then find the sum for each equation.

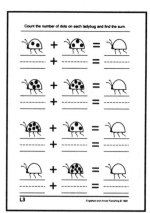

Make It, Man It, Move It

Objective Students will participate in an activity that plans, makes, and sells an original product.

Learning Outcomes Citizenship 10, 11, 12

Materials Grocery bags containing various materials available in the classroom such as cups, straws, lunch bags, yarn, crayons, markers, scissors, glue, etc.

Procedure Students will be divided into groups of three. Each student in the group will have a leadership responsibility for one activity either planning, making, or selling their product. Roles will be assigned by color chips: blue (planning), red (making), and yellow (selling) the product.

Groups will become "entrepreneurs" as they decide to make something using the materials found in their bags. The "planning" leader (blue) will make the final decision about WHAT to make; the "making" leader (red) decides HOW to make it; and the "selling" leader (yellow) decides the best way to let other people know about this great product.

Follow Up
1. How did your group decide what product to make?
2. What were some things that helped you decide what to make?
3. How did you decide tasks for each person in making the product?
4. How did you decide to sell your product?

Future Focus Students will explain and demonstrate their products to the class.

Circle Questions

	YES	NO
• Do you always buy gifts for special occasions?	O	O
• Have you ever made a special gift for someone?	O	O
• Have you ever sold something that you've made?	O	O
• Have you ever received a gift that was made for you?	O	O

Extend the Theme by Integrating Subjects

Writing
LO 4, 6

Have a brainstorm session to create a list of describing words that students can use to tell others about their products (for example: new, exciting, improved, fantastic) to create a table marker for a classroom Product Fair. Students can be encouraged to use magazines and newspapers to find words that will effectively describe and advertise their original products.

Mathematics
LO 11, 18

Students will set a price for the product that their group has made. The price will be $1.00 or less. Students will practice working with money amounts of $1.00, $.25, $.10, $.05, and $.01.

Citizenship
LO 10, 11

Students will try to identify the factors of production as applied to the products that each group has made. Divide the chalkboard into three categories:
- Land - refers to resources found in nature (i.e., leaves, acorns, stones)
- Labor - refers to the students making or selling the product
- Capital - refers to the man-made supplies in the product (i.e., markers, crayons, plastic cups)

Suggestion: The class can create symbols to identify each of the factors of production.

Student Poll – Fact or Opinion – Paper bags are better than plastic bags. Tally the results and compare viewpoints.

Science
LO 1

Provide a collection of items to classify as: Natural (from nature) OR Man-Made. Suggested items might include: paper clips, pine cones, plastic bags, real vegetables, grass, plastic fruits, or artificial flowers. As a class activity, students can place the objects into the correct category and explain the placement.

Safety Tip! Save natural resources by recycling.

Reading

Mighty Tree
Gackenbach, Dick
© 1992
Theme: different uses for trees for nature and people

The Picture Book of Kids Crafts and Activities
Henderson, Roxanne
© 1998
Theme: craft ideas

Englefield and Arnold, Inc. © 2000

Reading Continued

Good Earth Art
Kohl, Mary Anne F. and Cindi Gainer
© 1991

Craft Fun
Solga, Kim and Priscilla Hershberger
© 1997

Even More Stuff To Do!

- Visit a manufacturing plant to see a product produced from resource materials to a completed product (i.e., a candy factory).
- Create posters or bumper stickers to advertise the students' products.
- Equivalency - students can combine their coins to equal specific amounts. For example: If each student had ten pennies, how many students would need to combine their .01 coins to equal $1.00?

Teacher Notes

_____

_____

_____

_____

_____

Student Workbook Directions

M1   Student workbook page M1

Matching dollar values

Students will use a filled circle to indicate the price tag that correctly matches the price of each item listed: key, lunch box, pizza, tricycle, chair and toy dinosaur.

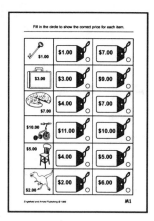

M2   Student workbook page M2

Identifying man-made objects and objects from nature

Students will use a filled circle to identify whether each item is man-made or from nature. The items listed include: an apple, a chair, a kitten, a car, a kite, a dandelion, and rocks.

M3   Student workbook page M3

Sequencing resource to product

Students will color and cut out the four pictures at the bottom of the page. Students will then paste the pictures in the correct order from resource to product:
1. lemons on the tree,
2. lemons picked from the tree,
3. lemons being made into lemonade, and
4. lemonade being sold.

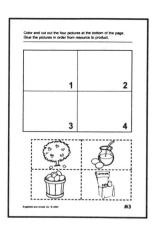

Next to Neighbors

Objective Students will understand that neighbor extends beyond the person living next door or the person sitting next to them.

Learning Outcomes Citizenship 4, 5

Materials
- crayons
- large piece of roll paper divided into four horizontal sections

Procedure Students will create a large pictograph. Divide a graph into the following categories:

   (1) Students that have lived in the school community their entire lives.
   (2) Students that have moved into the community from another city.
   (3) Students that have moved into the community from another state.
   (4) Students that have moved into the community from another country.

Each student will draw a picture of him/herself and place it in the correct category.

Follow Up
1. Who is your neighbor?
2. How many neighbors do you have in this classroom?
3. Are you a neighbor to anyone?
4. Does your classroom have a next door neighbor?

Future Focus Students can identify neighbors as people living beyond their home area.

Circle Questions

	YES	NO
• Does your best friend live in your neighborhood?	O	O
• Do your neighbors have pets?	O	O
• Do you have a new neighbor?	O	O
• Does your school have a neighbor?	O	O

Extend the Theme by Integrating Subjects

Writing
LO 1, 2, 3

Develop a list of words and phrases about being a good neighbor. Students can use the word and phrase list to complete the prompt using pictures or words: **A good neighbor is** _____.

Mathematics
LO 2, 10

Find the rule in an activity using ordered pairs. Students will recognize that numbers have neighbors too!

For example: 1,1   2,2   3,___   4, ___   5,5   6,6   (Find the rule.)
$$1+1, \quad 1+2, \quad 1+3, \quad 1+\underline{\quad} \quad \text{(Find the rule.)}$$

Citizenship
LO 13, 18

Discuss with students some responsibilities that we have to our neighbors. Topics might include: trash, noise, traffic, respecting laws.

Student Poll – Yes or No – A good neighbor always respects others. Tally the results and compare viewpoints.

Science
LO 16, 17

Extract a soil sample (near a tree trunk or water source like a pond or creek if possible) from outside. Using a jar large enough to hold a strainer, place the soil sample in the strainer. Put a light source (light bulb) directly over the jar for several hours (or overnight). The next day students might observe critters that have been drawn out of their cozy neighborhood.

Safety Tip! Light bulbs that are turned on can become very hot. Do not touch!

Reading

Meg and Jack Are Moving
Dowling, Paul
© 1990
Theme: moving

Good Luck, Ronald Morgan
Giff, Patricia
© 1996
Themes: communities; neighborhoods; neighborliness

Boy Who Wouldn't Speak
Berry, Steve
© 1992
Themes: giants; neighborliness; speech problems

Homer and the House Next Door
Pulver, Robin
© 1994
Themes: dogs; moving

Englefield and Arnold, Inc. © 2000

<u>A Country Far Away</u>
Gray, Nigel
© 1995
Theme: global neighbors

Even More Stuff To Do!

- Take a walk around the school's neighborhood.
- What things can your school do to be a good neighbor?
- Make a list of the restaurants in your town that represent neighbors from other countries and cultures.

**Teacher
Notes**

_____

_____

_____

_____

_____

_____

Student Workbook Directions

N1

Student workbook page N1

Students will recognize their faces as members of their school community, state, country and world.

Students will draw their own faces in the box that says "Me!" Students will then color and cut out the other pictures on the page. On a piece of 8 1/2" x 11" paper, students paste the pictures – one on top of the other – in the following sequence: globe, USA, Ohio, school, Me. Use this activity to discuss how the world is a universal community.

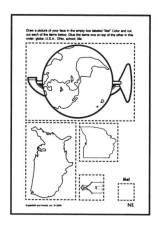

N2

Student workbook page N2

Identifying good neighborliness

This page includes four pictures of things that can happen between classroom neighbors. Three will be positive behaviors and one will be negative:
1. standing in line at the drinking fountain (positive)
2. helping the teacher clean the board (positive)
3. grabbing a ball from someone on the playground (negative)
4. carrying books for another student (positive)

Students will fill in the circles to identify the pictures that demonstrate good neighborliness.

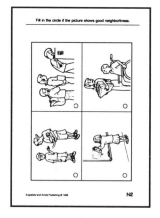

N3

Student workbook page N3

Students will supply the missing number neighbor in the sequence.

1, ___, 3, ___, 5, ____, 7, ____, 9, _____, 11, ____

___, 2, ___, 4, ____, 6, ____, 8, ____, 10 _____

10, ___, 12, ____, 14, ____, 16, ____, 18, _____

11, ___, 13, ____, 15, ____, 17, ____, 19, ____, 21

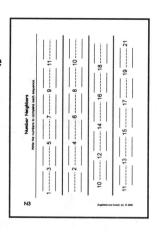

Once Upon a Time

Objective   Write and illustrate an original fiction story.

Learning Outcomes   Writing 1, 2, 3

Materials
- paper
- pencil
- crayons
- markers

Procedure   Using the prompt "Once Upon a Time" each student will write and illustrate an original fictional story using complete sentences (one sentence and illustration per page).

Follow Up
1. What type of story usually begins, "Once upon a time?"
2. What is a fiction story?
3. What is a nonfiction story?
4. How can you tell the difference between fiction and nonfiction stories?

Future Focus   Students are able to distinguish between fiction and nonfiction selections.

Circle Questions

	YES	NO
• Do you like to make up stories?	O	O
• Do you have a favorite "Once upon a time" story?	O	O
• Do you like fiction stories best?	O	O
• Do you like nonfiction stories best?	O	O

Extend the Theme by Integrating Subjects

Writing
LO 3, 4, 5

Develop a word list for each of the following categories: Character, Action, Setting. Students will then select one item from each category to illustrate the event. They can use pictures or words to accomplish this activity.

For example: The prince   walked   in the forest.
                (character) (action)   (setting)

Mathematics
LO 4, 5, 21

Use paper or plastic plates and markers to make a variety of analog (face) clocks to show time on the hour, quarter, and half-hour. Make a corresponding set of digital clocks representing the same times. Distribute an equal number of each type of clock to the students and ask them to find their matching partners.

Citizenship
LO 16

After reading a "Once upon a time" story to the class, students will look for information in the story that is true. Although "Once upon a time" stories are fictional, there can be many facts in them that are nonfictional, such as setting or character names. Students will compile a list of things that could be found true in a "Once upon a time" story.

Student Poll – Fact or Opinion – Fiction stories contain no true information. Tally the results and compare viewpoints.

Science
LO 2, 6, 7, 8

Using a stop watch or a clock with a second hand, students will predict how many jumping jacks or hops on one foot they can do in a given period of time (10 seconds, 30 seconds). Test their predictions.

Safety Tip! Do not overdo any type of exercising.

Reading

Once Upon A Time
Prater, John
© 1993
Themes: boredom; stories in rhyme
(Also by author: Once Upon A Picnic)

Once Upon A Time this Morning
Rockwell, Anne
© 1997
Themes: behavior; conduct; misbehavior; several short stories

Joe Giant's Missing Boot: A Mothergooseville Story
Gofee, Toni
© 1990
Themes: characters and characteristics; giants

Reading Continued

An Orange for a Bellybutton
Fukami, Harui
© 1988
Theme: giants

Hidden Treasures
Allen, Pamela
© 1986
Themes: imagination; creativity

Once I Was Very Small
Ferber, Elizabeth
© 1993
Theme: comparisons to being a baby

Dinorella
Edwards, Pamela Duncan and Henry Cole
© 1997
Theme: prehistoric fairytale

Time To...
McMillan, Bruce
© 1989
Themes: analog and digital time

Even More Stuff To Do!

- Visit a historical village for things that happened in the past.
- Visit a science museum to see how things or ideas have changed over time.
- Watch an animated film to distinguish fact from fictional information.

Student Workbook Directions

O1

Student workbook page O1

Time

Students will draw lines to match the digital times with the correct times on the clock faces.

1:00
2:15
3:30
4:45
5:00

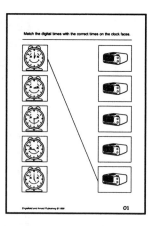

O2

Student workbook page O2

Once upon MY time. Estimate and check.

This page is a estimate and check sheet for aerobic activities. Students will estimate the amount of time they will be able to do each activity. Write in their guesses. Then, do each activity. Fill in the actual time after the activity is complete. Were their guesses greater or lesser than their actual times?

	guess	< = >	actual time
Standing on right foot			
Standing on left foot			
Standing on tip toes			
Running in place			
Jumping Jacks			

O3

Student workbook page O3

Complete the prompt

Students will color in the words "Once Upon a Time," then use pictures or words to describe a previous accomplishment or activity. For example, "Once Upon a Time... I learned to ride a bike, or went on a picnic."

Englefield and Arnold, Inc. © 2000

Pizza Puzzles

Objective

To separate whole number sums.

Learning Outcomes

Mathematics 5, 6, 11

Materials

- circle shapes (i.e., paper plates, pizza cardboards or construction paper)

Procedure

In this activity, students discover how separating whole numbers is just like adding toppings to a pizza. Ask the class to set the price for a cheese pizza (i.e., $3.00). Write the price on the several circle shapes. Next, set a price for each additional topping (i.e., $1.00/topping). Students will discover the price of various pizza combinations. For example, a pizza with two toppings will be seen as: $3.00 + $1.00 + $1.00 = $5.00.

Follow Up

1. How much would a pizza with four toppings cost?
2. How much would a pizza with three toppings cost?
3. How much would a pizza with six toppings cost?
4. How much would a pizza with a special topping for everyone in the class cost?

Future Focus

Students are able to separate whole numbers from one to twenty.

Circle Questions

	YES	NO
• Is pepperoni pizza your favorite kind of pizza?	O	O
• Do you have a favorite pizza topping?	O	O
• Is it likely that you would make pizza at home?	O	O
• Do round pizzas taste the same as square pizzas?	O	O

Extend the Theme by Integrating Subjects

Writing
LO 1, 2, 3

Write a letter to someone telling them how to construct a pizza (from crust to toppings) using pictures or words. Begin the letter with a greeting: **Dear ___,**

Mathematics
LO 7

Distribute a 9" x 12" sheet of manila or construction paper to each student. Direct students to fold their papers in half revealing two equal parts. What happens when the paper is folded in half again? How many parts have been created? Are they equal in size? How many parts are created if the paper is folded again?

Citizenship
LO 10, 11, 12

Have the class make a list of the products they think are used to make pizza. Accept lots of different logical suggestions. Explain that the maker of the pizza is a "producer" and the eater or buyer of the pizza is a "consumer."

Student Poll – Fact or Opinion – Everyone loves pepperoni pizza. Tally the results and compare viewpoints.

Science
LO 19

Examine the ingredients used to make a pizza such as tomatoes, cheese, different meats, and the crust. Find each ingredient on the food pyramid. (Food Pyramid found in Xtra-Xtra section, page 106.)

Safety Tip! Be careful when handling or eating hot foods.

Reading

Pete's A Pizza
Steig, William
© 1998
Themes: pizza; playing; imagination

Rocky Bobocky The Pizza Man
Ellison, Emily
© 1996
Themes: cooperation; mathematics; money; trading

Eating Fractions
McMillian, Bruce
© 1991
Theme: introduction to basic fractions

Ed Mouse Finds Out about Size and Shape
Head, Honor
© 1999
Theme: time and shape

Englefield and Arnold, Inc. © 2000

**Reading
Continued**

Pizza Soup
Robinson, Fay
© 1993
Themes: cooking; fathers and daughters; recipe; stories in rhyme

Little Nino's Pizzeria
Barbour, Karen
© 1987
Themes: fathers and sons; business; changes

Even More Stuff To Do!

- Visit a pizza parlor.
- Create a new pizza and send the suggestion (recipe) to a large pizza chain.
- Have a class pizza party.

Student Workbook Directions

P1

Student workbook page P1

Follow directions

Direct students to color the shapes on their pages according to the following direction key:
• Use your red crayon to color the pepperonis.
• Use your green crayon to color the peppers.
• Use your yellow crayon to color the mushrooms.
• Use your brown crayon to lightly color the crust.

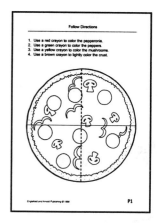

P2

Student workbook page P2

Introducing fractions

Students should cut out their pizzas from activity P1 — cutting along the outside (perimeter) of the pizza. Next, ask students to fold their pizzas in half along the dotted line and make a sharp crease. Reopen the folded pizza. Using a black crayon trace along the dotted line. Let students know that this line divides the pizza into two halves; each section represents 1/2. Now, have students fold their pizzas along the solid black line. Open the pizza back up and trace the new fold. Let students know that their pizzas are now divided into fourths. Each piece now represents 1/4.

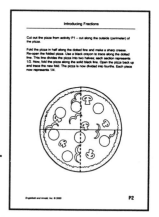

P3

Student workbook page P3

Circle survey

Each student will identify which pizza choice he/she prefers from the four categories: cheese, cheese + pepperoni, cheese + peppers, cheese + mushroom. All students should state their choices during a class poll. Students will listen while other students state their preferences. Each student will fill in a circle on his or her pizza poll for each choice that is stated aloud. Students will then write the total number of responses for each choice in the square. Students should compare results to see if everyone has the same graph information.

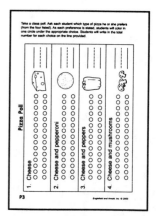

Quilt Quarters

Objective   Use a pattern of triangles and squares to create an Ohio Star quilt design.

Learning Outcomes   Mathematics 2, 7, 14

Materials   • the Ohio Star Quilt Pattern template
                    • poster board

Procedure   Draw a template design of the Ohio Star Quilt Pattern on a piece of poster board. (The template for this pattern can be found in the Xtra-Xtra section of this book, page 108 and Student Workbook, page Q1.) Cut out the 16 triangles and 5 squares for a total of 21 pieces. Next, draw the Ohio Star Quilt Pattern on the chalkboard or on another piece of poster board. Distribute the pieces to 21 students. Each student will match his/her piece to the pattern that has been drawn until the entire pattern is completed.

Follow Up   1. What two shapes are found in the Ohio Star design?
                    2. Can other patterns be made using only triangles and squares?
                    3. How many triangles did you find in each square?
                    4. How many different patterns did you make using your triangle and square shapes?

Future Focus   The class creates an original paper or material quilt. Display it in the classroom or hallway.

Circle Questions

	YES	NO
• Do you have a special blanket?	O	O
• Has anyone in your family ever made a quilt?	O	O
• Must all quilts be made from cloth (fabric)?	O	O
• Is it likely that all quilts are made with new fabric (cloth)?	O	O

Extend the Theme by Integrating Subjects

Writing
LO 1, 4, 6

Students will discuss special blankets or stuffed animals that they might have had when they were babies. Next, the class will brainstorm a list of words that describe their favorite things (i.e., fluffy, small, red and ragged).

Mathematics
LO 6, 8

Use workbook manipulatives from the quilt activity to represent problem solving. Students will color and cut out shapes to visualize number sentences. For example: Using three squares and three triangles, How many number sentences can be formed? 1 + 5 = ___, 2 + 4 = ___, etc.

Citizenship
LO 4, 5, 6

Discuss how quilt making is a historic art form. One Ohio culture group that makes and sells quilts is the Amish. The class might talk about different ways that people use quilts: blankets (keep warm) or wall hangings (decorations).

Student Poll – Fact or Opinion – Children always have favorite toys. Tally the results and compare viewpoints.

Science
LO 16

Demonstrate how plants and animals are alike in the things they need to live and grow. Make a list of the things that are needed to keep a living thing alive. Next to each item, place a "P" if it pertains to plants and an "A" if it pertains to animals. How many items have both a "P" and an "A?"

Safety Tip! Always be careful when using scissors.

Reading

Tar Beach
Ringgold, Faith
© 1991
Themes: Afro-Americans; Harlem; quilts

Luka's Quilt
Guback, Georgia
© 1994
Themes: grandmothers; Hawaii; quilts

The Keeping Quilt
Polacco, Patricia
© 1998
Themes: family generations; Jewish immigrants

Goodnight Hands: A Bedtime Adventure
Rozen, Michael J.
© 1992
Themes: bedtime; poetry; quilts

Even More Stuff To Do!

- As a class project, make a quilt out of cloth, and donate it to a children's hospital or a homeless shelter.
- Visit an Amish community in Ohio.
- Invite a relative (grandparent, aunt, uncle, etc.) to speak to the class about family heirlooms.
- Find other designs that combine basic shapes to create various quilt patterns.
- Laminate shapes and attach velcro for easy manipulation on a flannel board, or magnetic strips for manipulation on a magnetic board.

Teacher Notes

_____

_____

_____

_____

_____

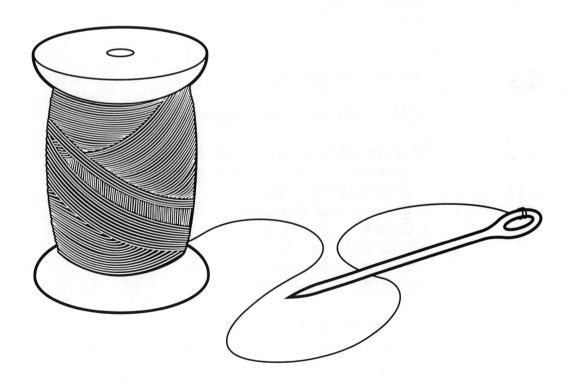

Student Workbook Directions

Q1

Student workbook page Q1

Ohio Star quilt pattern

Students will cut out the shapes using the cut lines indicated. Students should have a total of 16 triangles and 5 squares. These shapes can be manipulated to create original designs using only their triangles and squares.

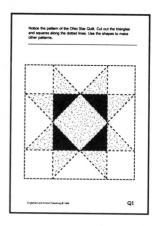

Q2

Student workbook page Q2

Using descriptive words

Develop a list of descriptive words that the class used to describe the blankets or stuffed toys they had as babies. Students will complete the sentences inside the teddy bear's tummy with words or pictures:

I had a special _____ when I was a baby.
It was _____.
It was _____.

Q3

Student workbook page Q3

Shape recognition/math manipulatives

Students will cut out the shapes after they have colored them according to the following directions:
- Color the triangles red.
- Color the squares purple.
- Color the circles blue.
- Color the rectangles yellow.
- Color the ovals orange.
- Color the diamonds green.

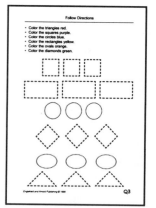

Students will use the shapes as manipulatives to practice and solve math problems. For example: 2 circles + 3 squares = 5 shapes

78

Englefield and Arnold, Inc. © 2000

Rootin, Tootin, Roots

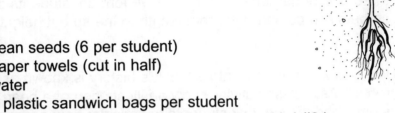

Objective   Students will learn through experimentation and observation about the function of roots in the life of a living plant.

Learning Outcomes   Science 5, 6, 8, 16

Materials
- bean seeds (6 per student)
- paper towels (cut in half)
- water
- 3 plastic sandwich bags per student
  (Label one bag #1, another #2, and the third #3.)

Procedure   Students will plant pocket gardens using the plastic bags, paper towels, and bean seeds. Put the same number of seeds in the packet that corresponds to the number on the outside of the plastic bag. Students will wrap the seed(s) inside a paper towel section, place inside the plastic bag and add enough water to wet the paper towel. Each student will have three packets to care for, observe, and record growth activity over a specific period of time.

Suggestion: If this activity begins on a Friday, some observable changes may take place over the weekend.

Follow Up
1. How many seeds did each student receive?
2. How many bean plants might you expect to get from each packet?
3. What will you need to do to help your seeds grow roots?
4. Do you expect all of your bean seeds to grow into mature bean plants?

Future Focus   Students are able to understand that plants are fed through their roots.

Circle Questions

	YES	NO
• Do all plants need roots?	O	O
• Do roots always grow below the ground?	O	O
• Do you like to eat beans?	O	O
• Have you ever planted a vegetable or flower garden?	O	O

Extend the Theme by Integrating Subjects

Writing
LO 1, 2, 3

Students will complete "I'm Rootin For You" awards by using the two carrot root shapes found in their workbooks (page R3). Students should state their reasons for giving the award. For example, "I'm Rootin For You because today is your birthday." The class might brainstorm a list of reasons for someone to receive a special award.

Mathematics
LO 17, 24

Students will measure and compare the lengths of the bean roots from their three pocket gardens. If sprouts have formed, students can measure the sprouts and compare the root length to the sprout height.

Citizenship
LO 3

Discuss why research into a family's history is known as "finding one's roots." As a class activity, show an illustration of a bean plant with roots, stems, and leaves. Ask students to consider how a family's roots (ancestry) can be compared to a bean plant. Who would be identified as the root system? (i.e., grandparents, great-grandparents) Who would represent the plant stem? The leaves? A family tree represents a family's time line.

Student Poll – Yes or No – Do you have any roots? Tally the results and compare viewpoints.

Science
LO 14, 16, 17

Suppose that a bean plant grew so tall that it reached into the clouds, similar to the plant in *Jack and the Beanstalk*. How might very large plants affect the environment? Do large plants have different needs than smaller plants to grow and stay alive?

Safety Tip! Plants need water to live.

Reading

The Rosey Fat Magenta Radish
Wolf, Janet
© 1990
Themes: imagination; vegetables

Potatoes
Turner, Dorothy
© 1988
Themes: nutritional value; recipes; crafts (nonfiction)

The Victory Garden Alphabet Book
Pallotta, Jerry and Bob Thomson
© 1992
Themes: good illustrations of root vegetables

Englefield and Arnold, Inc. © 2000

Even More Stuff To Do!

- Plant a root vegetable (beet, carrot, or radish) garden in the Spring.
- Creative writing: "The Bean That Took Over _____"
- Plant "mystery" seeds and predict what type of plant might develop. Is it a vegetable? Is it a flower? How tall will it get?

Teacher Notes

_____

_____

_____

_____

_____

_____

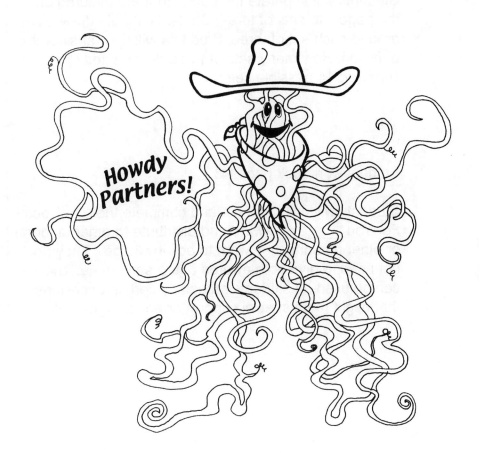

Howdy Partners!

Student Workbook Directions

R1

Student workbook page R1

Measurement

Students will use the table on page R1 to graph the length of their roots from the root growth activity on page 79. After the 10th day, students should carefully take out the plants from each of their three packets. Students will color in the number of boxes that correctly corresponds to the length of each root. How do the different roots compare?

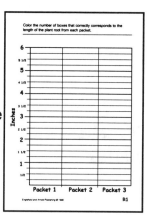

R2

Student workbook page R2

Beans in a bunch.

This page is covered with different kinds of beans. Students will separate the beans that are pictured on the page into sets of three. Students should draw a line around each set of three. Students will then answer the question: How many sets of three did you find? (Answer: 14 possible sets)

R3

Student workbook page R3

Students will color, cut out and complete the "I'm Rootin' For You _____" award and distribute to other students or other persons they want to acknowledge. They do not need to give both awards at the same time. These can be used as students recognize certain occasions that might merit special support or encouragement.

Sign Language

Objective   Recognizing signs and symbols that are used everyday.

Learning Outcomes   Reading 2, 12

Materials
- alphabet letters A-Z
- numerals 0-9
- weather signs
- safety signs
- paper
- crayons, markers

Procedure   Students will discuss common symbols which they may encounter on a daily basis: weather symbols, safety signs, speed limit signs. Early primary students should feel very privileged to know that by learning the 26 letters of the alphabet, they will be capable of reading and writing all of the words in the English language, and by recognizing and writing the symbols 0-9, they will be able to read and write all numbers in the Arabic System.

Follow Up
1. What other signs or symbols can you read?
2. What signs or symbols did you recognize or read at a very young age?
3. What does the + symbol mean to you?
4. What does the = symbol mean to you?

Future Focus   Students are able to read and follow directions when given various signs and symbols.

Circle Questions

	YES	NO
• Do you ever communicate without words?	O	O
• Have you ever used sign language?	O	O
• Is it necessary for you to read to know what a sign says?	O	O
• Can you talk to someone who cannot hear?	O	O

Extend the Theme by Integrating Subjects

Writing
LO 5, 9

Students will complete a 3-4 sentence rebus story (using a combination of words and pictures to tell a story). After completing the stories, ask students: "If you ONLY used pictures to tell your stories, would you be able to communicate your messages clearly?"

Mathematics
LO 3, 4,
8, 9

Students will recognize these basic math symbols +, -, =, <, >, as directions to complete a mathematic operation: + add, - subtract, = equals, < less than, > greater than. Decide which symbol is needed to complete each number sentence. For example: 3 ___ 1 ___ 4 (3 + 1 = 4) or (3 - 1 < 4).

Citizenship
LO 1, 15

- Discuss and rehearse safety procedures that the children will use in school: fire, tornado, emergency evacuation.
- Discuss how safety procedures are identified in the school.
- Safety codes (laws) are set up by local governments. Who might students expect to come to the school to oversee a fire drill?

Student Poll – Fact or Opinion – One picture is worth one hundred words. Tally the results and compare viewpoints.

Science
LO 2, 5, 13

Have students develop a two-week weather map using symbols found in the newspaper or created in class. This can be a daily documentation of the weather or a prediction of upcoming weather. If using the map for predictions, compare it against the actual weather conditions.

Safety Tip! It is important to have an evacuation plan at home.

Reading

Oh, How I Wish I Could Read!
Gile, John
© 1995
Themes: signs and symbols; safety; stories in rhyme

Even More Stuff To Do!

- Use magazines and advertisements to find pictures of fast food restaurant signs, sports emblems, logos, road signs, or product labels. Create a collage of signs and symbols students understand.
- Invite a sign language interpreter to the classroom.
- Invite a Music teacher to talk about the symbols used in teaching music.

Student Workbook Directions

S1   Student workbook page S1

Create a rebus story

Students are given five pictures:
1. tree
2. stop sign
3. sun
4. bike
5. student

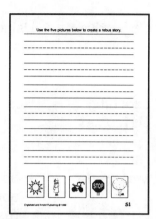

Each student will create a rebus story using words and pictures. Students might share and compare their stories to notice how even though the same words and pictures might be used, each person can create a unique story by using them in a different order.

S2   Student workbook page S2

Sequencing (Patterning)

Students will fill in the circle to indicate the next sign in the pattern.

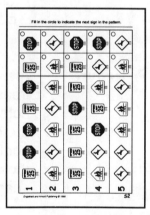

S3   Student workbook page S3

Categorization

Students will cut and paste the sign or symbol that should be included in each particular category. Five groups of symbols are shown:
1. weather signs (cloud, sun, rain)
2. alphabet letters (S, e, n)
3. numbers (6, 2, 8)
4. traffic signs (stop, traffic light, pedestrian crossing)
5. speed limit (35 mph, 20 mph, 50 mph)

Five symbols to be placed: snowflake, the letter 'A,' the number '9,' a deer crossing, and a 40 mph speed limit sign.

A Treasure of Tails

Objective   Using fiction and nonfiction books, stories, and poems, children will listen to, read and select reading materials about animals with tails.

Learning Outcomes   Reading 9, 19

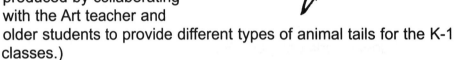

Materials
- books about animals
- gold covered treasure box (use gold paper or lame' fabric to cover a box)
- a variety of different animal tails made of yarn, paper, or fabric (These could be produced by collaborating with the Art teacher and older students to provide different types of animal tails for the K-1 classes.)

Procedure   After reading a variety of literature about animals, provide students with a treasure box containing pictures of various animal-type tails: monkey, cow, horse, alligator, lion, pig, fish, etc. Students may select tails from the treasure box and then look for (at home or in the school or public library) fiction or nonfiction picture books or story books about the animals that possesses those types of tails. For example, Lyle the Alligator or Curious George to share in class.

Follow Up
1. How do some animals use their tails?
2. Are animals able to communicate with their tails?
3. Is it necessary for an animal to have a tail?
4. Have you ever listened to a story called a tale?

Future Focus   Students are able to identify fiction and nonfiction books and stories.

Circle Questions

	YES	NO
• Is it a fact that all animals have tails?	O	O
• Would you ever need to have a tail?	O	O
• Are animal tails always long?	O	O
• Has anyone ever told you a tale?	O	O

Extend the Theme by Integrating Subjects

Writing
LO 1, 2, 3

As a class activity, develop a list of animals that have tails and ways these animals use their tails. Complete the following prompt using pictures or words: _____ **use their tails** _____. (<u>Dogs</u> use their tails <u>to show they are happy</u>.)

Mathematics
LO 2, 24

The class will construct a bar graph to record the animal books that have been read in class. The animals, rabbits, lions, monkeys, etc. can be represented with words or pictures. When a student finishes a book, he or she can fill in a block to designate the completion. Students might predict which animal will be the most popular in the class. Check the prediction when the data collection is completed to compare the prediction and the result. How long will the graph be kept? What estimations and future predictions might the class make using the graph information?

Citizenship
LO 8

After reading or listening to a story, book, or poem about a particular animal, indicate on a map (Ohio, United States, world) or a globe where that animal's natural environment (habitat) is located.

Student Poll – Fact or Opinion – All animal tails are beautiful. Tally the results and compare viewpoints.

Science
LO 14

Discuss with students the terms "extinct" and "endangered" relating to animals. What are some reasons that animals might become extinct or endangered. How do humans contribute to both protecting and endangering certain animals?

Science Tip! Our pets depend on us to take care of them.

Reading

Tom's Tail
Jennings, Linda M.
© 1995
Themes: pigs; self-perception; tails

Tat's Rabbit Treasure
Kerins, Anthony
© 1993
Theme: intriguing trunk and its contents

Very Mixed Up Animals
The Millbrook Press, Inc.
© 1998
Theme: flip book with mix and match animal parts

Paul Bunyan
Kellogg, Steven
© 1984
Theme: tall tales

Even More Stuff To Do!

- Make bookmarks in the shape of different tails to companion the stories the students have authored.
- Create a classroom library of student created stories and books.
- Send for a current list of endangered animals.
- Write letters to the editor to encourage protection of endangered animals.

Teacher
Notes

_____

_____

_____

_____

_____

_____

Student Workbook Directions

T1 Student workbook page T1

Writing

Students will write a tale about a lion on the lines provided.

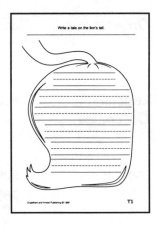

T2 Student workbook page T2

Comparison of size

Students will color the animal that correctly answers each question:

1. Which of these three animals is the longest?
   whale   frog   fish
2. Which of these three animals is the tallest?
   bear   deer   giraffe
3. Which of these three animals is the smallest?
   pig   cow   hen
4. Which of these three animals is the biggest?
   cat   horse   duck
5. Which of these three animals is the shortest?
   bird   dog   tiger

T3 Student workbook page T3

Students will compare sets of animals using > greater than, < less than, and = equal to. Remind the students to make the comparison from left to right. Students will designate their choice by filling in the circle of the correct answer.

For example: 3 frogs pictured   >   <   =   2 frogs pictured
                                   ●   o   o

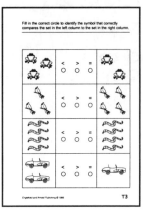

Under, Over, Around and Through

Objective   Students will listen to directions and navigate under, over, around and through terrain areas.

Learning Outcomes   Citizenship 7, 8

Materials
- scripted story (Teacher's Edtion, page 91)

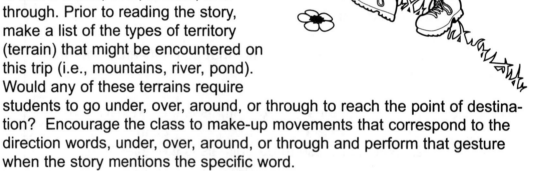

Procedure   Using the scripted story on the next page, students will be guided on an imaginary journey using the directional terms under, over, around, and through. Prior to reading the story, make a list of the types of territory (terrain) that might be encountered on this trip (i.e., mountains, river, pond). Would any of these terrains require students to go under, over, around, or through to reach the point of destination? Encourage the class to make-up movements that correspond to the direction words, under, over, around, or through and perform that gesture when the story mentions the specific word.

Follow Up
1. What might be some safety rules to follow when going on a hike?
2. Why are safety rules necessary?
3. Can we extend the journey by adding more directions?
4. What other types of imaginary trips could we go on?

Future Focus   Students can use a simple map key to recognize different terrains on a map.

Circle Questions

	YES	NO
• Would you usually hike around a mountain?	O	O
• Have you ever walked through a forest?	O	O
• Could you travel over Lake Erie?	O	O
• Is it likely that mountains are taller than hills?	O	O

Scripted Story

Today, we are going on a special imaginary journey together. Listen carefully while I read the directions that you are going to follow:

We are standing at the edge of a thick forest. The leaves on the trees are dark green. The wind is blowing just a little bit. The sun is shining very bright, and the day is warm. Can you hear the sound of the airplane's engine as it flies <u>over</u> our heads? Are you ready to begin the journey? The entrance to the forest lies between two tall trees. These trees guard the entrance like two stately giants. One tree is thick and smooth; the other tree looks old and shaggy.

Let's enter the forest. Be careful as you step <u>through</u> the narrow opening. The path <u>under</u> our feet is bare ground. Look <u>around</u> the forest, there are many tall trees. Many leaves and branches have fallen to the ground. Turn to the left, a raccoon is scurrying to a nest he made <u>under</u> a dead tree trunk. Think about the creatures that make their homes <u>under</u> the leaves and branches.

As we make our journey, the path <u>through</u> the forest is taking us <u>around</u> a large rock. Think about other things you might see in the forest: a deer, an old shed, wild mushrooms, or squirrels. What might you see on the floor of the forest: a penny, an arrowhead, unique stones? Notice, there are lots of spots where green grass is growing on the ground, but no grass is growing on the path. A little piece of blue sky is peeking <u>over</u> the treetops. Look out! There's a low branch straight ahead - duck <u>under</u> the branch. Notice how a vine has wrapped itself <u>around</u> the branch.

As we walk a few steps more, we come to an area in the forest that is very thick. The sun does not shine <u>through</u> the trees in some spots. If you look <u>around</u>, way into the forest, it is almost black. The forest is dark, and we hope there is enough light to see the path. Because the forest is so dense with trees and plants, we will not be able to walk anywhere but on the path.

Oh no! We have a problem. Several fallen trees - almost four feet high - are blocking the path. How can we get to the path on the other side of this obstacle (roadblock)? How will we continue our journey? Maybe we should turn back and head for home?

[At this time, discuss with the class possible answers to the questions that were just posed. Assuming the class makes the decision to cross over the obstacle, continue with the story.]

Back on the path, we travel for a few more minutes. The trees aren't quite so thick anymore. We can see the blue sky again. Looking up, we see the birds flying <u>over</u> the forest. There is a pond in the distance. The pond is down a small hill. As we get closer to the pond, we can see that a rope bridge has been built <u>over</u> the water. The path does continue <u>around</u> the pond. Should we walk across the bridge or take the path? Should we turn <u>around</u> and go back? How should we decide what to do? What information might affect the decision making?

[At this time, discuss the answers to the questions that were posed. As a class, decide whether or not you should continue. If they decide to continue, ask for their help in making-up the next leg of the journey. Don't forget to mention points where students must go <u>over, under, around, or through</u>.]

Extend the Theme by Integrating Subjects

Writing
LO 1, 2,
3, 5

Students will respond to and create additional "What if...?" prompts using pictures or words:
- What if my school was located in the middle of an island?
- What if I lived in a treehouse?
- What if ...?

Mathematics
LO 12, 13,
20

Acquaint students with geometric terms: perimeter (around), parallel (over and under), intersecting (through) lines, and interior (inside) and exterior (outside). Use the six basic shapes: circle, square, rectangle, diamond, oval, and triangle. Provide specific directions. For example: Draw a red line around the perimeter (outside) of each shape, color the interiors of the shapes green, etc.

Citizenship
LO 1

Use the "What if...?" prompts to discuss cause and effect relationships. "What if the fire bell rang now?" We would follow the firedrill procedure and evacuate the building. What is the cause? What is the effect?

Student Poll – Yes or No – It is possible to go over a forest. Tally the results and compare viewpoints.

Science
LO 11, 14,
15

Conduct a simple experiment to demonstrate erosion (wearing away of the land). Demonstrate erosion by using a small bottle to spray a mound of dirt with water. Discuss what might cause water erosion and discuss ways to prevent it. Ask students to make observations and predictions about the effect of water erosion on the land's surface. Students might hypothesize how the amount and force of the water can have further complication (i.e., flooding).

Safety Tip! Do not assume that all liquids kept in spray bottles are safe for children to use.

Reading

Over, Under and Through
Hoban, Tana
© 1973
Theme: directions

Down in the Subway
Cohen, Mirian
© 1998
Theme: an imaginary trip

Englefield and Arnold, Inc. © 2000

Reading Continued

Outside, Inside
Crimi, Carolyn
© 1995
Theme: opposites

I Took a Walk
Cole, Henry
© 1998
Theme: a trip in the woods

Even More Stuff To Do!

- Look for and identify different types of terrain, landforms, and bodies of water, on a map of Ohio, a map of the United States, or a world map.
- Students can conduct other erosion-type simulations.

Student Workbook Directions

U1

Student workbook page U1

Follow directions

Students will guide the rabbit through the park using the following directions:
1. The rabbit hops through the tunnel.
2. The rabbit runs around the tree.
3. The rabbit hops under the swingset.
4. The rabbit climbs up the slide ladder.
5. The rabbit goes down the slide.
6. The rabbit hops across the sandbox and finds his carrot.

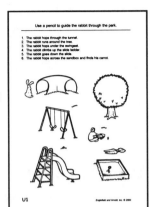

U2

Student workbook page U2

Recognize opposite words

Students will look at the pictures in the left column and fill in the circles to identify opposite word partners.

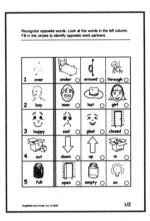

U3

Student workbook page U3

Follow directions

Students will color the scene according to the following directions:
• The fish swims through the river. Color the fish orange.
• The river is under the bridge. Color the river blue.
• The cattails are around the river. Color the cattails green.
• The bridge is over the river. Color the bridge brown.
• The sun is over the bridge. Color the sun yellow.

Varoom – Visible Vocabulary

Objective   To observe and identify different ways that writers use words to attract a reader's attention and interest in books, stories, or poems.

Learning Outcomes   Reading 4, 14

Materials
- a variety of books, stories, and poems demonstrating different writing styles

Procedure   Students will listen to and/or read several different types of books, stories or poems and begin to notice how an author uses language in his/her writing to capture a reader's attention. Some examples may include: rhyming, repeated words or phrases, onomatopoeia, descriptive words, etc.

Follow Up
1. Do you have a favorite book, story, or poem?
2. Is there a special author that you like?
3. What are some things that authors do to attract your interest to a book or story?
4. What can you do, as an author, to attract the interest of your readers?

Future Focus   Students are able to recognize ways that some authors use vocabulary in literature.

Circle Questions

	YES	NO
• Are you an author?	O	O
• Do you usually like stories that rhyme?	O	O
• Do you ever use words that make sounds?	O	O
• Do you always use special sounds when you play?	O	O

Extend the Theme by Integrating Subjects

Writing
LO 4, 6, 7

Students will create their own writer's reference books. Create a word list of nouns (naming words), adjectives (describing words) and verbs (action words). Students should use these references to help with different writing activities throughout the year. These lists will grow as the language development of the class increases.

Mathematics
LO 3, 10

Mathematics has a vocabulary that all students must learn. Not only must they recognize the word form for numbers, they must also interpret math symbols and know the vocabulary that corresponds to those symbols. Create a mathematics vocabulary list of words and symbols that represents the concepts being taught (i.e., number names: one, two, five, or addition: plus, equals).

Citizenship
LO 4, 5, 6

People come to Ohio from many different places in the United States and different countries in the world. Are students able to identify words that we use in the English language that might have come from a different country? What about words that identify certain foods associated with different ethnic groups: taco, pizza, sauerkraut.

Student Poll – Yes or No – All ethnic groups prepare food the same way. Tally the results and compare results.

Science
LO 10

- Demonstrate the operation of some simple machines (pulley, wheel, axle, wedge, inclined plane, or screw). Ask students to suggest toys that have simple machines incorporated into them. Different areas for them to consider include: an inclined plane on a toy car race track, a bicycle, toys with wheels.
- Discuss whether or not simple machines make work easier or more difficult. To illustrate this point, ask students what sounds they would make if they were pushing a heavy object up an incline without the aid of a simple machine? Would they make a different sound if their efforts weren't so difficult? What made the task easier: the simple machine.

Safety Tip! Always use equipment properly.

Reading

Elbert's Bad Word
Wood, Audrey and Dan
© 1988
Theme: language usage

Englefield and Arnold, Inc. © 2000

Reading
Continued

Invasion of the Giant Bugs
Woods, A. J.
© 1996
Themes: vivid language; holograms

Goodness Gracious!
Cummings, Phil
© 1989
Themes: vocabulary; adjectives

Suddenly!
McNaughton, Colin
© 1994
Theme: word use

Yum!
McNaughton, Colin
© 1998
Theme: word use

Super, Super, Superwords
McMillan, Bruce
© 1989
Theme: comparisons

London Bridge is
Falling Down, Falling Down...

Even More Stuff To Do!

- Invite the Music teacher to teach the students "rounds" or songs with repeated verses.
- Learn some dance steps, using fast and slow music.

Teacher
Notes

_____

_____

_____

_____

_____

_____

Student Workbook Directions

V1

Student workbook page V1

Matching

Students will match the equations: words to numerals
1. four plus one equals five   10 - 3 = 7
2. three minus two equals one   5 + 4 = 9
3. ten minus three equals seven   9 - 3 = 6
4. six plus two equals eight   3 - 2 = 1
5. five plus four equals nine   4 + 1 = 5
6. nine minus three equals six   6 + 2 = 8

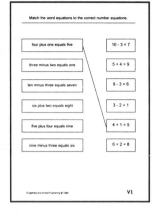

V2

Student workbook page V2

Complete the following sentences using describing words (adjectives), naming words (nouns), or action words (verbs).

1. I rode my bike to the _____.
                                        (noun)

2. My mom made _____ for my family.
                          (noun)

3. The _____ balloon floated in the air.
              (adjective)

4. The _____ _____.
         (noun)   (verb)

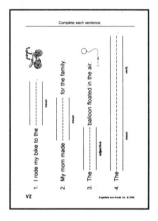

V3

Student workbook page V3

Punctuation

Students will fill in a circle to identify the punctuation mark (. ? !) that completes each sentence:
1. We won the game!
2. Do you ride the bus to school?
3. I went fishing on Saturday.
4. Are you going to the library today?

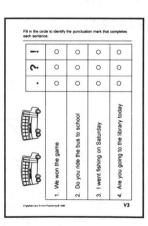

Who, What, Where...?

Objective Students learn sentence construction and summarizing using question cues: who, what, where.

Learning Outcomes Reading 1, 5, 14
Writing 3, 4, 5

Materials • Wendell the Whale template (Teacher's Edition, page 111 and Student Workbook, page W3)

Procedure Use the table tent featuring Wendell to introduce the students to Wendell a "wondering whale" who questions everything. Who? What? Where? Students will learn to construct simple sentences when reminded of Wendell's wondering (questioning) ways. After reading a short story, ask the students to develop wondering questions about the story such as:
• **What** is the story about?
• **Who** is a main character in the story?
• **What** does the main character do in the story?
• **Where** does the story take place?

Follow Up 1. Who is Wendell?
2. How can Wendell help students?
3. Where should students keep Wendell when composing sentences?
4. How will Wendell be helpful to students in both reading and writing?

Future Focus Students are able to construct sentences. Each sentence follows a logical beginning, middle and end.

Circle Questions

	YES	NO
• Do you think Wendell is a good name for a whale?	O	O
• Do you like to ask questions?	O	O
• Do you always get your questions answered?	O	O
• Do whales live in Ohio?	O	O

Extend the Theme by Integrating Subjects

Writing
LO 9

Wendell reminds students that he is a V.I.W. (Very Important Whale). He wants to remind students that a name always begins with a capital letter. Whenever Wendell writes, he always begins sentences with capital letters and ends each sentence with a punctuation mark.

Mathematics
LO 17

Select one type of whale and have students draw a lifesize model on the playground with chalk. Create a template with large roll paper using the actual measurements of a specific type of whale or create one based on student estimation and suggestion. After tracing around the template, the children can use rulers, yardsticks, or other measuring devices to determine the length and height of the whale.

Citizenship
LO 13, 17, 18

Using a picture book about whales, discuss with students that the government has certain laws that protect whales. What might be some reasons that whales need protection? Brainstorm a list of reasons that students have suggested to protect whales.

Student Poll – Yes or No – Laws always protect people. Tally the results and compare viewpoints.

Science
LO 1, 16

What do whales need in order to live? Compare and contrast a goldfish and a whale, determining what is needed for each to live. Use a Venn diagram (page 107) to demonstrate how a goldfish and a whale can have shared and different characteristics.

Safety Tip! All living things must be fed regularly.

Reading

Students can begin identifying main character(s) - who, action (plot) - what, setting - where, and theme - why or how in books and stories using Wendell's "wondering" cues.

Whale Is Stuck
Hayles, Karen and Fuge, Charles
© 1992

Whale
Allen, Judy
© 1992
Theme: includes whale factsheet

Whale Song
Johnston, Tony
© 1987
Themes: whale songs; 1-10 counting

V.I.W.

Very
Important
Whale

Even More Stuff To Do!

- Could Inspector Inch grow as a result of telling fish stories (tales)?
  Write a fiction story or a tale using Inspector Inch as the main character.
- Check out nonfiction books about whales from the library.
- What causes animals to become endangered or extinct?
- Find the measurements for a larger or smaller whale and have students
  recreate it themselves in the same way that they did the first one.
  Perhaps they can work in smaller groups and make a school of whales.
- Write a letter to the Environmental Protection Agency requesting
  information about the protection of whales.

Teacher Notes

_____

_____

_____

_____

_____

_____

Student Workbook Directions

W1

Student workbook page W1

A simple dichotomous key

Students will fill in a circle to indicate which animal(s) each sentence applies to: a goldfish, a seal, a whale.
- (1) I live in water.
- (2) I can live in a small bowl.
- (3) I cannot live in a small bowl.
- (4) I use my fins as feet.
- (6) I do not use my fins as feet.

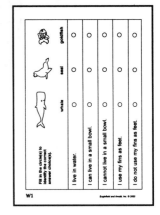

W2

Student workbook page W2

The students will cut out the four sentences at the bottom of the page. Read one sentence. Do any of the parts of the sentence answer these questions: Who? What? Where?

Cut up the sentence and paste the parts of the sentence that answer a particular question in that column.

For example: The team   won the game.
              (paste under who)   (paste under what)

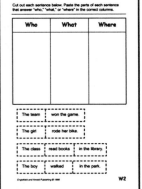

W3

Student workbook page W3

Wendell the Whale is featured on the workbook page. Students are to cut along the dotted lines and fold along the solid line to make a table tent to aid during sentence construction. There are three questioning words that have emerged from Wendell's spout. Students should color these questions according to these directions and use Wendell to help construct sentences.
- Who? (square)   yellow
- What? (triangle)   red
- Where? (circle)   blue

Xtra! Xtra!

Teacher Resources
All sites active at time of publication.

Blue Web'n Content Categories
This website, provided by Pacific Bell Education First, links to exceptional educational websites they have rated. The websites are categorized by subject area and type.
http://www.kn.pacbell.com/wired/bluewebn

Puzzlemaker
Need a crossword puzzle, word search or some other kind of puzzle? Come to this site, plug in your words, and a puzzle will be generated for you to print out and use.
http://puzzlemaker.school.discovery.com

SOITA (Southern Ohio Instructional Technology Association)
A list of sights, arranged by subject, recommended by member teachers and SOITA staff.
http://www.soita.esu.k12.oh.us/resources.html

Eisenhower National Clearinghouse
A thorough site for science and math educators: national standards information; journal articles; lesson plans; project ideas; resources and links to other science and math sites.
http://www.enc.org

Free-Federal Resources for Educational Excellence
Free federal resources for educational excellence. A searchable listing of federally supported, Internet-based education resources.
http://www.ed.gov/free

TeachWeb
Provides links to many different subjects as well as to newsletters and classified ads.
http://www.teacherweb.net

Skill-Building Games
A site that provides games for skill-building.
http://www.funbrain.com/

Internet Public Library: Reading Zone
Features a directory of links to reading related sites. Early elementary students can read folktales along with a narrator.
http://www.ipl.org/youth/

Classroom Resources
All sites active at time of publication.

The Children's Literature Web Guide
An Internet resource related to books for children and young adults. Includes links to authors, book reviews, bulletin boards, and quick reference lists.
http://www.acs.ucalgary.ca/~dkbrown/

Discovery Channel Online
The Discovery Channel presents this online version of their programming. A variety of topics covering current events, social studies and science are presented. The site also includes live camera views of several animals in zoos across the nation.
http://www.discovery.com

Exploratorioum
Science is more than just fun at the exploratorium-it's meaningful! Learn about the science behind everyday events with interactive activities and web videos!
http://www.exploratorium.edu

Grandpa Tucker's Rhymes and Tales
In the words of Grandpa Tucker, "Here are funny stories that deliver a message, silly poems that will bring a smile and allow you to share some thoughts."
http://www.night.net/Tucker

I'm A Kid
This site shows some of the articles from Weekly Reader Magazine and is a good place to go if you like to take part in polls or enjoy sharing your opinions about different topics.
http://www.weeklyreader.com/features/kid.html

World of Reading
If you are looking for some books by a favorite author, or want to do a search on a title of a book, come to this site. You'll get a review of the book submitted by other young readers. Students can even submit their own reviews!
http://www.worldreading.org

Earth Preservers
Environmental news, information and puzzles for students, teachers and parents.
http://www.earthpreservers.com

Some More Great Picture Books!

One Hundred Is A Family
Ryan, Pam Munos
© 1994
Themes: various family units; counting 1-10, 10s to 100.

When A Line Bends A Shape Begins
Growler, Rhonda
© 1997
Themes: mathematics; shapes

Sweet Clara and the Freedom Quilt
Hopkinson, Deborah
© 1993
Themes: slavery; quilts; map

Would You Rather...
Burningham, John
© 1978
Theme: choices

Thinking Like a Scientist

Questions for students to consider while conducting experiments:

- What do I want to know?

- What do I think might happen?

- What steps will I use to find out?

- What really happened?

- What did I find out?

Food Pyramid

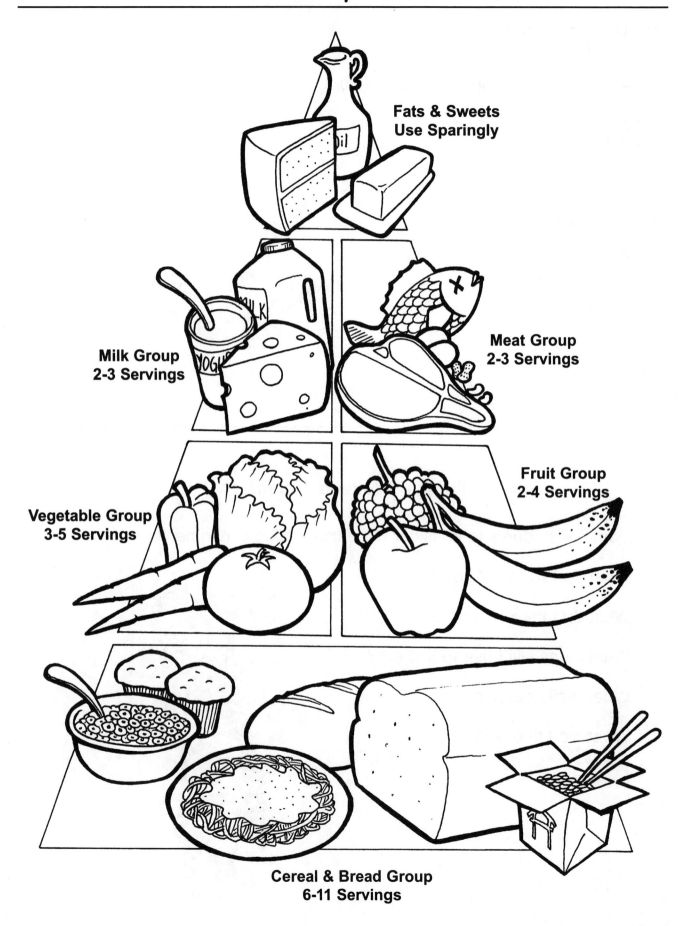

Fats & Sweets
Use Sparingly

Milk Group
2-3 Servings

Meat Group
2-3 Servings

Vegetable Group
3-5 Servings

Fruit Group
2-4 Servings

Cereal & Bread Group
6-11 Servings

Student Poll

Tally the number of responses.	
Yes	
No	

Tally the number of responses.	
Fact	
Opinion	

Belongs to Group A   **Belongs to Group B**

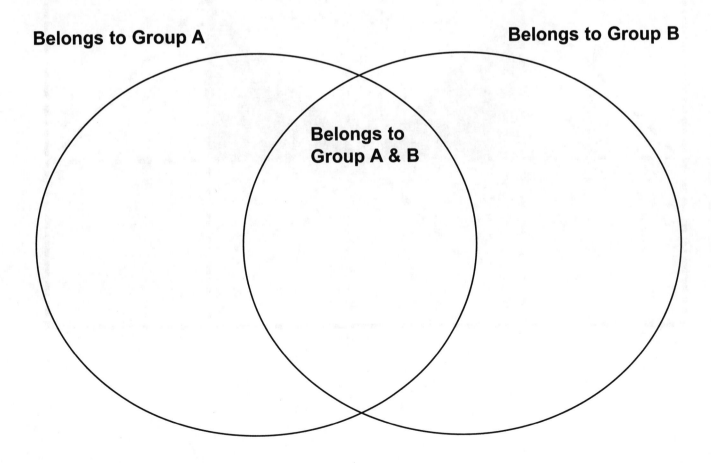

Belongs to
Group A & B

Ohio Star Template

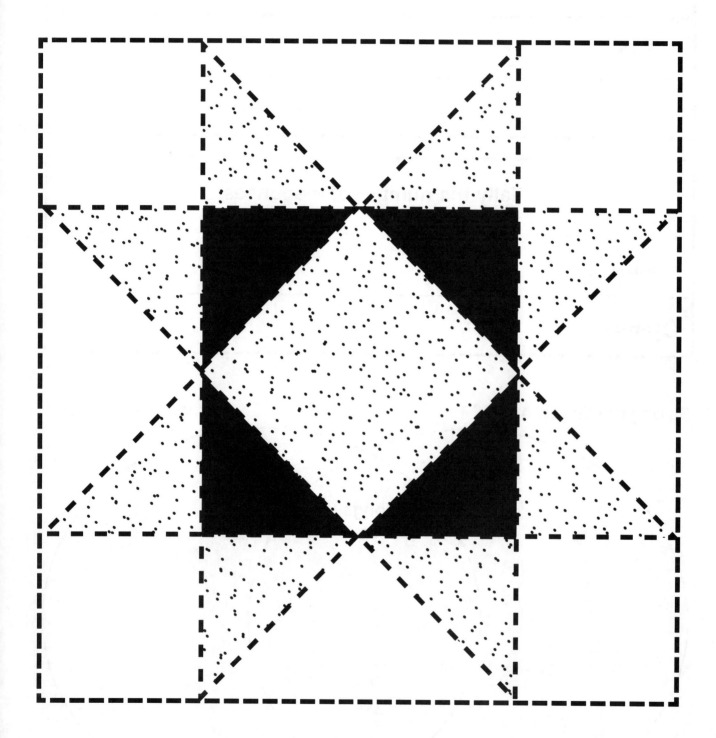

Matching Cards for Lucky, Lucky Ladybug Activity

Each student will need one sheet.

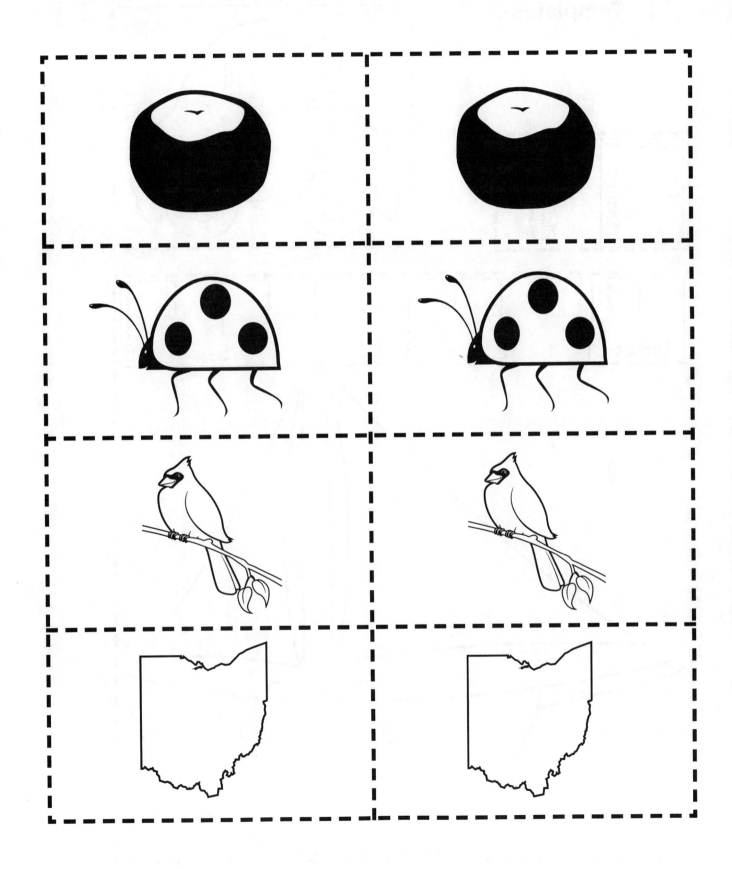

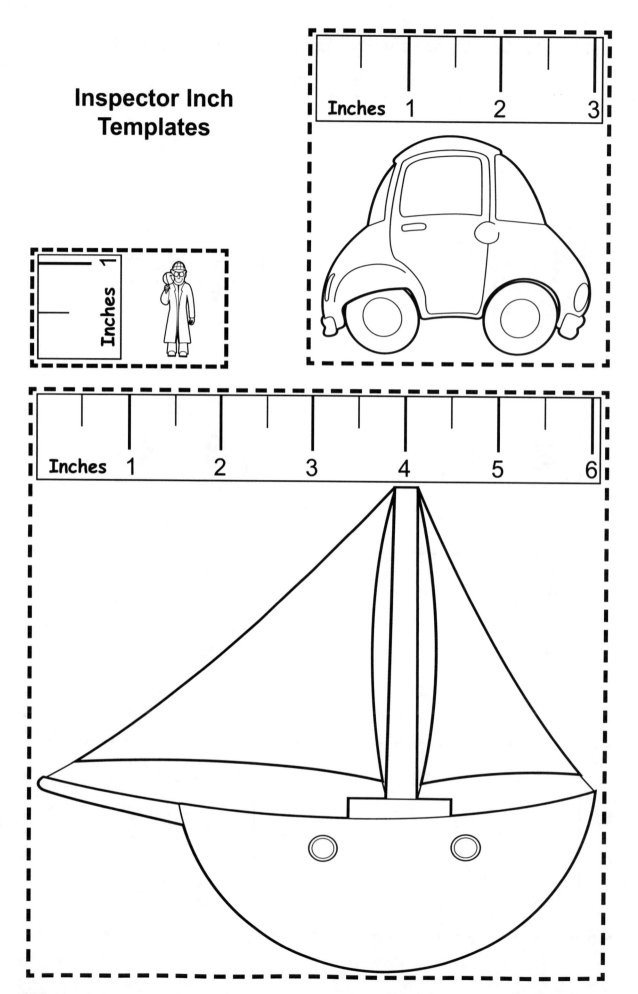

Inspector Inch Templates

Inches 1 2 3

Inches 1

Inches 1 2 3 4 5 6

Wendell the Whale table tent template.

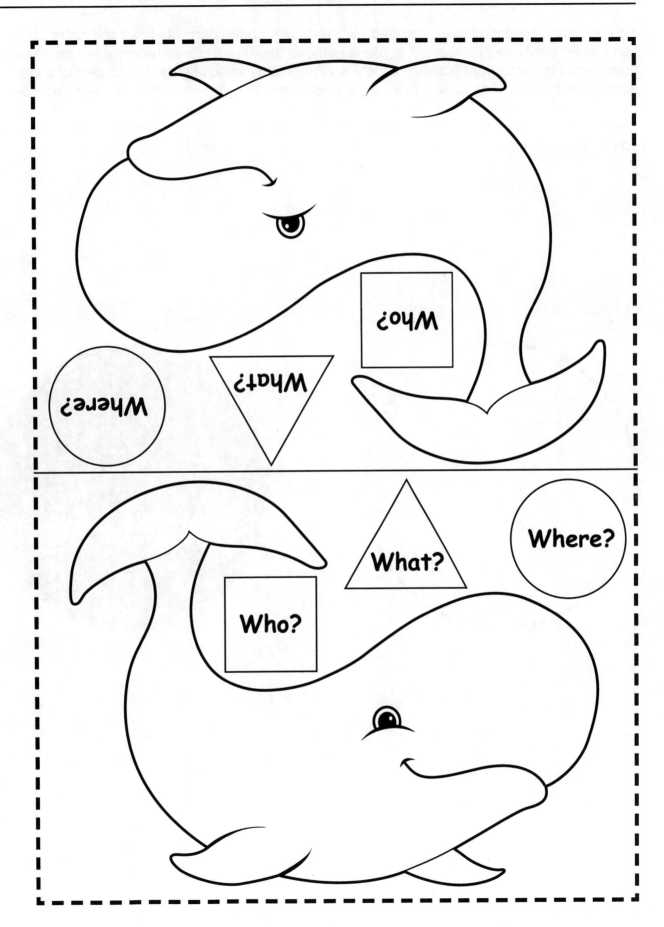

Circle Question Paddle Pattern

The open and filled circles will be used over and over again, particularly for the circle questions found under each lesson. It is recommended that these circles be mounted on heavier paper and laminated for durability. Create one paddle by attaching the two circles to a craft stick, back-to-back. The paddle presents a closed circle on one side and an open circle on the other side. Students will become familiar with the idea that filled circles represent their answer choices (i.e., on the Ohio proficiency test, multiple choice questions are answered by completely filling in the circles).

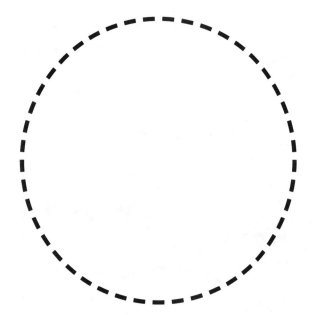

Yikes! Yeast!

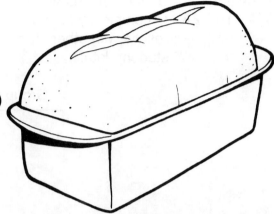

Objective Students will make observations and inferences over time.

Learning Outcomes Science 6, 11

Materials
- a package of yeast (1/2 teaspoon)
- 1/4 cup of warm water
- baby food jar
- 1/2 teaspoon sugar
- chart to record predictions

Procedure Students are shown the ingredients that will be used in this demonstration (or experiment if students will be doing it). Encourage students to make predictions about what might happen during every step of the process. Check for changes every 10 minutes. Changes will include bubbles, foam and an odor. The steps include:
1. Pour the yeast into the clear glass jar.
2. Add water to the yeast.
3. Add sugar.
4. Make observations.

Using a clock with a second hand, students can time the number of minutes it takes for a noticeable change to happen, the container to fill up completely, and for the yeast to stop growing.

Follow Up
1. Can you explain what happened to the yeast?
2. Did you expect this reaction?
3. What might happen if more yeast were used?
4. What did the sugar do to the yeast?

Future Focus Students are able to identify simple physical changes.

Circle Questions

	YES	NO
• Have you ever helped someone make bread?	O	O
• Does bread dough need sugar in it?	O	O
• Must all breads have yeast as an ingredient?	O	O
• Are all sandwiches made with bread?	O	O

Extend the Theme by Integrating Subjects

Writing
LO 1
Create a class book. Each student will contribute an individual page about, "The Yeast That Grew and Grew and Grew."

Mathematics
LO 4, 19, 24
Use teaspoons and tablespoons to determine how many of each it will take to completely fill a baby food jar with water. Have students compare their results with other students in the class. Complete the following chart with student data:

Group #	Teaspoon/Jar	Tablespoon/Jar

Citizenship
LO 4, 6
Some culture groups are identified with special types of bread. Students can "taste" the diversity of Ohio's cultural groups by sampling some different breads. Relate each type of bread with a particular group: pita (Greek), tortilla (Mexican), matzah (Jewish). Students might contribute by sharing bread that is related to their family's culture.

Student Poll – Fact or Opinion – Rye bread tastes good. Tally the results and compare viewpoints.

Science
LO 17
Make a list of five or more things that are affected by temperature changes (i.e., water, animals) and give an explanation for each using pictures or words.

Safety Tip! Take special care of outside pets during extreme temperature changes.

Reading
Peanut Butter and Jelly
Wescott, Nadine Bernard
© 1987
Theme: a play rhyme

Even More Stuff To Do!

- Use a bread maker to make bread in the classroom.
- Use group decision making to select the type or flavor of bread to make. Notice how the aroma will penetrate the room and the school.
- Is there a connection between the sense of smell and the sense of taste?

Englefield and Arnold, Inc. © 2000

Student Workbook Directions

Y1   Student workbook page Y1

Identification of living things

Students will fill in the circle to identify which of the following
are living things: tree, boot, ladybug, bird, car, squirrel, flag,
flower, bike.

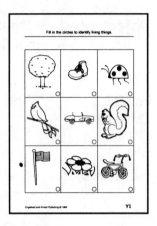

Y2   Student workbook page Y2

Making observations

Students will observe fishbowl A and fishbowl B. Students will
write three things that are the same.

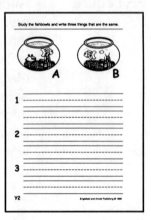

Y3   Student workbook page Y3

Cut and paste to solve riddles

Students will use this cut and paste activity to select one of the
measuring instruments – thermometer, stopwatch, ruler, measuring cup – to answer each riddle.

1. I can be used to measure flour for making bread.
   What am I?

2. I can be used to measure inches and centimeters.
   What am I?

3. I can be used to check the temperature.
   What am I?

4. I can be used to time a race.
   What am I?

Zany zAnimals

Objective   Create an original animal and write a story about it. The story will model a nonfiction book about an animal.

Learning Outcomes   Writing 1, 2, 3

Materials
- pencils
- paper

Procedure   After becoming familiar with nonfiction animal books and the kind of information that is included in these books, students will write their own books about the animals that they have created. Each new animal should have a unique name. Some information for their books may include: a description of the animal (i.e., color, size, does it resemble another animal), what it eats, where it lives.

Follow Up
1. Could any animals share the same living space (habitat)?
2. Is your animal able to live anywhere?
3. Would your animal make a good pet?
4. Does your animal like to be around humans?

Future Focus   Students can write nonfiction information in a fictional story.

Circle Questions

	YES	NO
• Have you ever been to a zoo?	O	O
• Do you believe that lions are kings?	O	O
• Is an elephant bigger than a hippo?	O	O
• Do all animals have four feet?	O	O

Extend the Theme by Integrating Subjects

Writing
LO 1, 6
Students can brainstorm a list of action phrases that describe how animals move (i.e., slither like a snake or hop like a rabbit). Students will select one action to pantomime for the class to interpret.

Mathematics
LO 18
Students will work with dimes and nickels to figure the cost of pet supplies. Give specific information about the amount of different supplies needed and the cost of each item. For example, if one can of dog food costs one dime, how many dimes will you need to purchase two cans of dog food? If one cat toy costs one nickel, how many nickels will be needed to buy four toys?

Citizenship
LO 13, 18
Discuss with the students whether animals have or should have rights guaranteed by the government? What rights should animals have? Who should protect these rights? Make suggestions for a law that could be written for animals.

Student Poll – Fact or Opinion – Animals should have rights. Tally the results and compare viewpoints.

Science
LO 14, 17
Talk about how animals need to adapt and adjust to new circumstances and situations:
• What happens to some animals when housing developments are built and their habitats are destroyed?
• What happens to some animals when there is a flood or a forest fire?
• What happens to some animals when the seasons change?
• What other things might affect how animals adjust to different environments?

Safety Tip! Never approach strange animals.

Reading
<u>Very Mixed Up Animals</u>
The Millbrook Press, Inc.
© 1998
Theme: flip book with mix and match animal parts

<u>The Mixed Up Chameleon</u>
Carle, Eric
© 1975
Theme: change

Student Workbook Directions

Z1

Student workbook page Z1

Match the animal to its habitat.

Students will draw a line to match the animals to their habitats.

fish   pond
bird   tree
snake   grass
deer   forest
ladybug   flower
spider   spiderweb

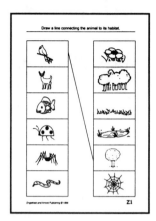

Z2

Student workbook page Z2

You have been left to care for the neighbor's pets and special instructions are given for you to buy a certain number of items each day. Fill in the circle to indicate the correct price for each item.

bag of carrots $.10 each
dog biscuits $.25 each
bag of birdseed $.15 each
jug of milk $.20 each
box of fishfood $.05 each

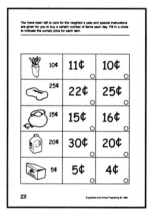

Z3

Student workbook page Z3

Follow directions

Students will color each animal. Next, students will cut the thick dotted lines. Remind them to be careful not to cut outside the designated lines. Students will then fold along the solid lines to create a variety of unusual animals by interchanging heads, bodies, and feet.

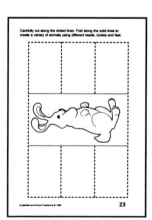

Now available for grades K-12: proficiency test preparation materials – books, flash cards, and software! See reverse side for order form.

Questions?
Call Englefield & Arnold Publishing's Accounting Department
Monday through Friday, 9 am to 5 pm, toll free at 1-877-PASSING

Phone Orders
Before you call, complete the product order form on the next page. Please have your credit card number or school purchase order number available.

Call toll free: 1-877-PASSING (727-7464).

Mail Orders
Photocopy and complete the product order form on the next page. Schools should attach purchase order to product order form. Mail to:

Englefield & Arnold Publishing
P.O. Box 341348
Columbus, Ohio 43234-1348

Fax: (614) 764-1311
Photocopy and complete the order form on the next page. Schools should fax purchase order with product order form. If purchase order is mailed separately, please write "DO NOT DUPLICATE" on purchase order.

Individual Orders
Orders from individuals cannot be invoiced. Orders must be accompanied by a personal check or money order with full payment, or charged to Visa, Mastercard or Discover (including tax and shipping costs).

Tax
Ohio tax applies to all non-exempt customers. Please add 5.75% to your total. If your order is tax exempt, you must submit a tax exemption certificate.

Preview Copies
Free preview copies of some materials are available to school administrators. Requests for previews must be faxed or mailed on school letterhead. If you are interested in previewing materials, call the Sales and Marketing Department, toll free, at 1-877-PASSING.

Shipping
Please use the following chart to calculate shipping charges and add it to your total.

Qty	Rate	Qty	Rate
1-2	$4.00	11-15	$8.00
3-5	4.50	16-20	10.00
6-8	5.00	21-29	14.00
9-10	6.00	30 +	4%

Shipping

Most orders can be processed within 48 hours. Shipping usually takes 7-10 days.

Returns**
To insure a full credit, contact the Accounting Department (1-877-PASSING) to obtain a return authorization number. No returns are accepted without a Return Authorization Number. Send authorized returns to:

Englefield & Arnold Publishing
6344 Nicholas Drive
Columbus, Ohio 43235

** Item(s) must be returned in resellable condition within 30 days of purchase.

Quantity Discounts*
Schools can receive quantity discounts on large orders. See chart below.

Quantity	Discount
1 – 29	0%
30 – 49	10%
50 – 199	15%
200+	20%

Quantity Discounts

* Discount does not apply to already discounted classroom sets, lab packs, site licenses, and the newsletter.

119

Englefield & Arnold Publishing • P.O. Box 341348 • Columbus, OH 43234-1348

PH (614) 764-1211 • 1-877-PASSING (727-7464) • FAX (614) 764-1311 • Internet: www.eapublishing.com

Ship To ATTN:	Bill To ATTN:
School/Business:	School/Business:
Address:	Address:
City: State: Zip:	City: State: Zip:
Phone: ( )	Phone: ( )

Grades K-1

Qty	Item	Description	Price	Total
	102	Teacher Edition	16.95	
	103	Student Workbook	10.95	
	199	Classroom Set	275.00*	

4th Grade Products

Qty	Item	Description	Price	Total
	404	Teacher Edition	16.95	
	405	Student Workbook	10.95	
	406	Answer Key Booklet	3.00	
	407	Classroom Set	275.00*	
	412	Mathematics Flash Cards	10.95	
	413	Citizenship Flash Cards	10.95	
	414	Science Flash Cards	10.95	
	415	Reading/Writing Flash Cards	10.95	
	426	Software - Version 2.0	39.95	
	426L	Software/Lab Pack (5 CDs)	149.95*	
	425S	Software/Site License (30 CDs)	599.95*	

6th Grade Products

Qty	Item	Description	Price	Total
	601	Teacher Edition	16.95	
	602	Student Workbook	10.95	
	603	Answer Key Booklet	3.00	
	699	Classroom Set	275.00*	
	604	Math Masters	29.95	
	612	Mathematics Flash Cards	10.95	
	613	Citizenship Flash Cards	10.95	
	614	Science Flash Cards	10.95	
	615	Reading/Writing Flash Cards	10.95	
	626	Software - Version 2.0	39.95	
	626L	Software/Lab Pack (5 CDs)	149.95*	
	626S	Software/Site License (30 CDs)	599.95*	

9th Grade Products

Qty	Item	Description	Price	Total
	900	Student Book	16.95	
	912	Mathematics Flash Cards	10.95	
	913	Citizenship Flash Cards	10.95	
	914	Science Flash Cards	10.95	
	915	Reading/Writing Flash Cards	10.95	
	926	Software - Version 2.0	39.95	
	926L	Software/Lab Pack (5 CDs)	149.95*	
	926S	Software/Site License (30 CDs)	599.95*	

12th Grade Product

Qty	Item	Description	Price	Total
	1200	Passing with Honors	24.95	

The Ohio Proficiency Press™ Newsletter (4 issues per year)

Qty	Item	Description	Price	Total
	100	Newsletter subscription	14.00*	

Method of Payment:

___   Check/money order   Ck # _____

___   Purchase Order   P.O. # _____

___   Tax Exempt   Tax I.D.# _____

___   Credit card: ___ Visa ___ M/C ___ Discover

Card #: _____

Expiration Date: _____ / _____

Signature: _____

Total Ordered	
Quantity Discount*	
Tax (5.75%)	
Shipping	
Total Due	

Quantity Discounts

Qty	Discount
1 – 29	0%
30 – 49	10%
50 – 199	15%
200 or more	20%

Shipping

Qty	Rate	Qty	Rate
1-2	$4.00	11-15	$8.00
3-5	4.50	16-20	10.00
6-8	5.00	21-29	14.00
9-10	6.00	30 +	4%

* Discount does not apply to already discounted classroom sets, lab packs, site licenses, and the newsletter.

Prices Subject to Change